A New North America

A New North America

Cooperation and Enhanced Interdependence

Edited by
Charles F. Doran
and Alvin Paul Drischler

Westport, Connecticut
London

Library of Congress Cataloging-in-Publication Data

A new North America : cooperation and enhanced interdependence / edited by Charles F. Doran and Alvin Paul Drischler.
p. cm.
Includes bibliographical references and index.
ISBN 0–275–95406–4 (hc : alk. paper).—ISBN 0–275–95407–2 (pb : alk. paper)
1. Free trade—North America. 2. North America—Foreign economic relations. 3. North America—Economic integration. 4. Free trade—North America—Public opinion. 5. Public opinion—North America. I. Doran, Charles F. II. Drischler, Alvin Paul.
HF1746.N49 1996
337.1′7—dc20 95–40576

British Library Cataloguing in Publication Data is available.

Library of Congress Catalog Card Number: 95–40576
ISBN: 0–275–95406–4
0–275–95407–2 (pbk.)

First published in 1996

Praeger Publishers, 88 Post Road West, Westport, CT 06881
An imprint of Greenwood Publishing Group, Inc.

Printed in the United States of America

The paper used in this book complies with the Permanent Paper Standard issued by the National Information Standards Organization (Z39.48–1984).

10 9 8 7 6 5 4 3 2 1

Contents

Acknowledgments

Appreciation goes to the William H. Donner Foundation (U.S.) for its generous support of the North American Studies Program of the Nitze School of International Studies, Johns Hopkins University, which has underwritten this volume. Thanks are especially due to James Capua, President of the Donner Foundation (U.S.), and to William Alpert, the Executive Director, both of whom have exercised great vision regarding North American regionalism. The board members of the Donner Foundations have taken a deep, positive interest in these efforts throughout.

Also extremely helpful have been Bernardo Sepulveda-Amor, former Foreign Minister of Mexico; Robert Kasten, former U.S. Senator from Wisconsin; and Tom Axworthy of the CRB Foundation in Montreal, who together have chaired policy discussion sessions for the project. Meetings in Washington, D.C., Mexico City, and Toronto have strengthened the argument and evidence of these chapters, specially prepared for this volume.

Abbreviations and Acronyms

AFDC	Aid to Families with Dependent Children
AFL-CIO	American Federation of Labor and Congress of Industrial Organizations
AFTA	ASEAN Free Trade Area
ASEAN	Association of South East Asian Nations
BIS	Bank for International Settlements
CACM	Central American Common Market
CARICOM	Caribbean Common Market
CBI	Caribbean Basin Initiative
CET	Common External Tariff
CUFTA	Canada-U.S. Free Trade Agreement (same as FTA)
EC	European Community
ECLAC	Economic Commission for Latin America and the Caribbean
EFTA	European Free Trade Association
EITC	Earned Income Tax Credit
EPA	Environmental Protection Agency
ESF	Exchange Stabilization Funds
EU	European Union
EZLN	Zapatista Army of National Liberation, Mexico
FDI	Foreign Direct Investment
FDIUS	Foreign Direct Investment in the United States
FTA	Free Trade Agreement, Canada and United States (also called CUFTA)
G-3	Group of Three (Mexico, Colombia, Venezuela)
GATT	General Agreement on Tariffs and Trade

GDP	Gross Domestic Product
GIS	Guaranteed Income Supplement
GNP	Gross National Product
IBWC	International Boundary Waters Commission
ICS	International Coordinating Secretariat
IFI	International Financial Institutions
ILO	International Labor Organization
IMF	International Monetary Fund
LAC	Latin America and Caribbean
MERCOSUR	Southern Common Market (Argentina, Brazil, Paraguay, Uruguay)
MFN	Most Favored Nation
MOU	Memorandum of Understanding
NAAEC	North American Agreement on Environmental Cooperation
NAALC	North American Agreement on Labor Cooperation
NACE	North American Commission on the Environment (U.S.-Mexico)
NAFTA	North American Free Trade Agreement
NAO	National Administrative Offices
NDI	National Democratic Institute
NED	National Endowment for Democracy
NGO	Non-Governmental Organization
OAS	Old Age Security
OECD	Organization for Economic Cooperation and Development
PAN	Party of National Action, Mexico
PRD	Party of the Democratic Revolution, Mexico
PRI	Institutional Revolutionary Party, Mexico
RCTC	Refundable Child Tax Credit
SSI	Supplementary Security Income
USAID	U.S. Agency for International Development
WHFTA	Western Hemisphere Free Trade Area

Introduction: After NAFTA

Charles F. Doran

What will North America look like after NAFTA? That is the analytic challenge which the authors in this volume have undertaken to examine. The North American free-trade area encompasses a population of over 370 million people. Its total annual gross domestic product in U.S dollars is 6.7 trillion. Three-way trade exceeds 270 billion U.S. dollars annually, making it equal in trade and commercial terms with the two other "economic power centers" in the world, the European Union and South and East Asia. Although the numbers are impressive, they do not tell the whole story. The real, underlying question is, Where is the North American region going? How strongly do Mexico, Canada, and the United States identify with the region? What strategies exist to propel North America into the twenty-first century?

To get at some of these questions, the book divides the analysis into two parts.

The first part considers the perspectives of each of the three countries toward the region and toward the problems each faces in adapting to structural change brought about, to varying degrees, by regionalism. This section of the book also highlights the expectations each society possesses regarding the benefits of increased trade, investment, communication, and interpersonal and institutional contact within North America. The conclusions surprise. Each polity holds very different expectations. Moreover, the positive expectations within each country are themselves mixed. Foreboding over what may have to be given up colors the optimism regarding what may be gained. A tenacious realism seems to result.

If the hopes for economic benefit from regionalism are correspondingly higher for Mexico and Canada than for the United States, the fear of adjustment is also far greater in those two countries. But what perhaps stands out in all three countries is how hard-fought the free-trade vote was, how entrenched the industrial and labor opposition was, and how great a political leadership was necessary to get the U.S.-Canada Free Trade Agreement and NAFTA passed. In none of these polities did the regional free(r) trade option sweep through easily. In Mexico, for example, the greater political centralization facilitated enactment of the NAFTA, but the high-level assassinations that followed revealed the extent of the inner political tensions surrounding the decision to open up economically.

Hence the task in the first section is not only to discriminate among the three countries in terms of political and economic outlook, but also to separate the fears associated with regionalism in each country from the sense of genuine promise.

In the second part of the book, the analysis moves from present circumstance and expectations to strategy and options. On the conceptual plane, the NAFTA in some ways was the easy answer. At least its membership and essential parameters were quite certain. The road to "enhanced interdependence," or to fuller economic integration and efficiency, is not so simply demarcated. Rather, there are forks in the road as well as unsuspected bends, and even some anticipated rough patches ahead. What the highway builders of North American regionalism perhaps need most is a few good surveyors who can take the lay of the land and give the highway engineers, as well as the future drivers, a feeling for what lies ahead.

A fundamental quandary regarding future options and strategy is whether, to use the language of regionalism, to "widen" or to "deepen" first, and how to do it. This quandary is not made any easier by the experience of the European Union (EU), where the desire is to move forward to political union. Notwithstanding that desire, the members of the EU still cannot muster enough coherence to achieve monetary union, let alone a single foreign policy. In North America the objective is quite clearly not to move toward political union. But the members of the free-trade area nonetheless want greater market efficiency. Somehow the efficiency is to be purchased at no loss of sovereignty to any of the three states. This is a tall order.

Nor is the evolution to higher levels of economic integration in North America without countertrends in each of the three polities. The idea of decentralization of administration and policy implementation appeals to constituents in all three countries. Yet how are "rules-of-origin" agreements and customs management to occur without some greater centralization of rules? Trade dispute resolution mechanisms are just one further piece of evidence on behalf of the reality that greater market efficiency requires some concessions in terms of the respective national sovereignties. Perhaps the greatest apparent antinomy here between evolution and devolution is the Parti Quebecois government in Quebec, which wants full independence from Canada (devolution) combined with full membership in NAFTA (evolution). This second section attempts to sort out all of these apparent conundrums, while advocating new strategies and options to achieve enhanced North American interdependence.

PERSPECTIVES FROM THREE COUNTRIES

Delal Baer opens the volume with a sobering appraisal of the challenges that face Mexico in the wake of the NAFTA. Not only has violent rebellion occurred within one subregion, Chiapas, but two top members of the governing party have been assassinated over boiling tensions that stem at least indirectly from the adjustments, political and economic, facing all Mexicans. She leaves the impression that expectations of benefit in terms of growth are very high, not only in governing circles but throughout much of the society. She also implies that the society politically will not be ready for much more immediate economic change brought about by external agreement until the consequences of reform have begun working their way through labor hall and boardroom.

Edward Safarian concludes that Canada faced a much rougher time in digesting the consequences of the U.S.-Canada Free Trade Agreement than Canada has had with the consequences of NAFTA. This differential experience is to be explained by the respective size of the trade figures. Eighty percent of Canada's trade is with the United States. NAFTA primarily affected only about 2 percent of Canada's trade, that with Mexico. Yet Canada has contemplated another problem with North American market integration. The North American market may be one, but Canada's own market remains quite balkanized. Moreover, Canadians wonder what impact further North American interdependence will have on their own prospects for retaining a sense of Canadian cultural identity, on the one hand, and for retaining sufficient political unity across the whole of Canada, on the other.

Quite in contrast to some of these expectations and worries, Alvin Drischler notes surprising findings for the United States. Many analysts in the United States did not expect very much from greater North American market integration. Indeed, the alarmists—and they were a large and noisy group—predicted just the opposite: substantial loss of firms. Led by Ross Perot, who popularized the notion of the "giant sucking sound" of investment leaving the United States for Mexico, the alarmists played on the fears of U.S. citizens that the United States would be relatively worse off after the creation of a free-trade area instead of better off. But Drischler's essay demonstrates exactly the contrary. NAFTA has been a boon to investment, both new investment coming from abroad, especially from Japan, and new investment that has been generated at home in anticipation of intensified growth. Hence U.S. citizens who doubted the merits of North American integration may find themselves the unwitting beneficiaries of significantly higher economic growth and employment because of membership.

We are thus confronted with three very different country perspectives. Mexicans know that North American integration will benefit them in the long run. They did not anticipate how rocky the politics would be in the short run. Canadians went along with NAFTA mostly as a defensive measure to prevent a "hub-and-spokes model" from emerging in which they were a mere spoke. While the economic benefits of increased North American economic rationalization are likely to be very real for Canada, which like Mexico will enjoy a much higher overall economic growth than the United States, Canada is entering a struggle for its very existence as a unified country. North American market integration may be good for Canada. But just as a dip in the Atlantic may be good for one's "constitution," so regional integration may be helpful to Canada if Canada's Constitution survives the bracing swim.

The United States may come out the big winner, at least a bigger winner, than even the proponents of North American integration envisioned. Much depends upon the flow of international investment. But what seems clear at the moment is that this investment is not coming at the expense of either Mexico or Canada. Rather, the investment being attracted to the North American marketplace is new investment, investment that is coming here or staying here because the North American marketplace looks dynamic, more dynamic than without NAFTA. As with much of life, economic growth can become a self-fulfilling promise. With new investment will come a stronger flow of trade within the region, much of it intra-industry and intra-firm, thus driving the overall three-nation dynamic faster and further.

POLICY OPTIONS AND ENHANCED INTERDEPENDENCE

According to the basic proposition argued in the opening piece of the second section, on strategy and options, widening (addition of new members) and deepening (concentration on policy harmonization and standard-setting) follow a sequence. Deepening ought to precede widening, because widening adds diversity, and diversity leads to conflict over priorities and goals. By widening first, a regional entity is likely to forgo certain aspects of deepening, since insufficient agreement will exist in the larger trade area to pursue the goals of deepening, or at least to pursue them with enough vigor to achieve greater market efficiency. Conversely, deepening can be pursued first without the sacrifice of widening, inasmuch as other governments in the region will always be prepared to join a large, powerful new trade grouping essentially on its own terms, as the European experience surely suggests.

Clearly, Charles Doran is making the case for a review of the strategy of regional development. He claims that this strategy cannot be based just on the pure economic model of Viner or of Balassa. Rather, he believes that political judgment is essential to the formulation of a strategy of region-building. A valid strategy for regional development is all the more critical where political union is not the goal, and where supranational institutions will not exist, to bolster the movement toward greater regionwide market efficiency, an efficiency that necessarily includes deepening as one of its principal vehicles.

Keith Banting takes a bold look at what a strategy of deepening means. His main vantage point is the matter of convergence or divergence of policies. He finds that Canada and the United States have so far diverged on many social policies and converged only on a few. Convergence on child benefits results, he says, from "parallel domestic trends" rather than from any kind of reciprocal influences. Though more contentious, especially in its Canadian regional application, unemployment insurance in both countries has converged considerably over the years.

Banting notes that, regarding policy harmonization, what has happened in the past may not determine what will happen in the future. Some greater convergence of tax policies may be expected, for example. Issues in the public policy area, he says, tend to ebb and flow in terms of emphasis. Enhanced interdependence could see a unilateral review of some policies critical to market efficiency that will have the effect of multilateral movement. Banting leaves open the question of how much policy harmonization the three governments can or will want to achieve through direct negotiation.

Whether the side agreements on environmental cooperation and on labor problems are a step in the direction of greater market efficiency in trade and investment terms, or are meant primarily to promote these issues independently of their effects on economic efficiency, is a delicate question. Rafael Fernandez de Castro and Claudia Ibarguen explore these matters from a Mexican point of view. One of the problems here is the Mexican concern, understandable from their domestic perspective, to exploit their labor-cost advantage fully through regional economic arrangements. How much resistance to the regional trade area by U.S. and Canadian labor is due to fear of lower-cost competition, and how much is based on genuine concerns about Mexican labor conditions and labor practices—regarding child labor, for example—remains open to judgment. Likewise, the extent to which environmental groups recognize that economic growth is essential to the interests of all three communities is subject to debate.

What is rather evident is that the initiatives taken through the creation of the International Boundary Commission and the North American Agreement on Labor Cooperation have the effect of highlighting these issues over others in regional terms. These initiatives also force policymakers in all three countries to acknowledge that these priorities are parallel in character and cannot be pursued in such a way that one objective is sought at the cost of another. Such a recognition is a large step toward greater policy harmonization. On the other hand, the really difficult part is not the will to harmonize and to push labor standards and environmental betterment forward. The most difficult part is finding the resources at a time when neither Canada nor the United States is prepared to transfer much capital to the poorest partner.

Sidney Weintraub takes an essentially pragmatic and positive look at all of these options and strategies. He favors widening, but he thinks that at present Chile is really the only viable candidate for membership in the NAFTA. He is sympathetic to the need to deepen regional integration in North America and fully aware of the constraints on doing so in Mexico at a time when so much change is already being incorporated into business practices. He distinguishes between "strong" and "weak" regionalism and concludes that U.S. preferences here are likely to be key. Customs procedures may become much more important, he predicts, than is so far realized, determining whether co-production and just-in-time inventory techniques really take hold industrially in all three countries. Rules-of-origin problems and like difficulties could become the pretext for considering whether NAFTA should move beyond a trade area to the status of a common market.

Weintraub urges economists to study the problem of investment and trade diversion that is possibly associated with North American regionalism. He holds open the possibility that "concentric circles" of trade liberalization could occur in North America, just as in Europe. This approach could speed association without diluting the level of liberalization already achieved and without denying membership to countries that are more politically receptive to membership than they are economically ready for it. In general, Weintraub provides some guidelines as to who should be admitted as a member, how fast expansion of NAFTA should proceed, and what priority issues the architects of North American regionalism should now address.

Authors in the second section of the book seem to agree broadly about strategies and priorities. Weintraub and Doran, for example, agree that, as Weintraub says, "NAFTA should give itself time to deepen." Likewise, the Canadian and Mexican contributors note that analysts in both countries are beginning to identify policies and standards that are at variance with the efficiency sought regarding competitiveness within the overall North American market. Not the least of these tasks is the need to break down intra-country provincial and state barriers of a nontariff sort that hinder the movement of goods and services. Perhaps, for example, it is time throughout North America to establish tougher rules regarding the effort to use subsidies to promote localized investment.

Kenichi Ohmae echoes what is perhaps only the latest functional argument in favor of economic regionalism, when he talks about the "regional state."[1] If, he says, the object is to further the economic welfare of the individual within the society, then this can be done only by creating the economic conditions within the society that will attract the enterprise capable of increasing wealth for that individual. The nation-state is too small to do this any longer, even a nation-state the size of the United States. Regional states, or conglomerations of states, on the other hand, are large enough to permit the full specialization of labor, and the full economies of scale, to optimize the output of the firm. This is not the equivalent of "making the nation-state safe for the firm," to paraphrase an old, much-criticized Wilsonian adage regarding the world and democracy. It is the equivalent of making the firm maximally productive for the individual living inside the regional state.

This book is prudent, and at the same time imaginative, about the prospects for North American regionalism. Nowhere are the problems of achieving this goal minimized. But, likewise, nowhere are the authors hesitant to confront the obstacles to greater market efficiency that will constrain prosperity for the individual citizen in Mexico, Canada, and the United States. On the threshold of the twenty-first century, North America is in the process of creating a single market. Where we are, and where we want to be, are different things. This book attempts to bring the reality and the ideal, the present and the future, closer together.

NOTE

1. Kenichi Ohmae, "The Rise of the Regional State," *Foreign Affairs* (Spring 1993): 78-87.

PART I

PERSPECTIVES FROM THREE COUNTRIES

1

The New Order and Disorder in U.S.-Mexican Relations

M. Delal Baer

HARVEST OF HATRED

The image of Mexico cultivated in the Western press by the government of Carlos Salinas de Gortari (1988-94) was that of a country prepared to leap into the first world. No other president in modern Mexican history was so press and image conscious or so internationally oriented as Salinas. But dreams of first world splendor now contrast brutally with a string of calamitous third world nightmares, from guerrilla movements and assassinations to revelations of high-level government involvement in drug trafficking. A sense of disillusionment and economic breach of contract inevitably followed among those who believed in and invested in the dream. Did Mexico really fall so far, or did it dream too high?

Mexico, unique among the countries of the Western Hemisphere, suffered an unprecedented series of political blows that undermined economic stability. Salinas believed that he had cleared the most perilous political hurdles of his term by the close of 1993—the U.S. House of Representatives approved the North American Free Trade Agreement (NAFTA) on November 17, 1993, and the Institutional Revolutionary Party (PRI) nominated Luis Donaldo Colosio as its candidate for president without mishap on November 28, 1993. Then an obscure guerrilla movement declared war on the Mexican army, attacked five cities, repudiated NAFTA, and called for Salinas' resignation in the southern state of Chiapas on January 1, 1994. The PRI presidential candidate, Luis Donaldo Colosio, was assassinated the day following his reconciliation with political rival and Chiapas negotiator Manuel Camacho Solis, on March 23, 1994. Prominent business leaders were kidnapped in April, and the August presidential elections took on a polarized, threatening hue. The September assassination of PRI Secretary-General Jose Francisco Ruiz Massieu, and the spectacular accusations of PRI complicity made by his brother, Special Prosecutor Mario Ruiz Massieu, unsettled financial markets once again. By the time Ernesto Zedillo was inaugurated on December 1, 1994, the nation's financial stability had been hollowed out by successive political traumas.

Especially disturbing were the few clues to explain the violence or to clarify what thread, if any, unified those acts. Mexico resembled Plato's cave—one saw the shadows on the wall, but the hand that held the knife remained invisible. In the absence of institutional transparency, effective investigations, and hard information, Mexicans were gripped by an obsession with conspiracy theories and foreign investors assumed the worst. Almost all Mexicans believed that violence was being employed in a calculated fashion by unseen interests to tip the balance of political forces and protect criminal interests. Many speculated that Colosio's murder was engineered by hard-line enemies of political reform (*dinosaurs*) or drug interests opposed to judicial transparency. Others believed that the Chiapas uprising was a ploy by the radical Left to discredit market economic policies and tip the presidential election. Salinas and other major political figures became objects of suspicion as the impression spread of a submerged internal war conducted by obscure forces to achieve unnamed purposes.

President Zedillo named Antonio Lozano of the opposition party of National Action (PAN) as Attorney General, and by March 1995 he began to unravel the mysteries of the 1994 assassinations. The fact that the sources of destabilization were so close to the heart of government in the case of the Ruiz Massieu murder, with the arrest of Raul Salinas (brother of President Salinas) and former Deputy Attorney General Mario Ruiz Massieu (brother of Jose Francisco Ruiz Massieu), implied a chilling merger of economic/criminal interests and political power. It suggested competing political circles within the previously monolithic single party (the PRI), each with possible ties to Mafia-like interests.

Mexico is hardly unique with regard either to the pervasiveness, scale, or quasi-institutionalized style of corruption and narco-politics. Nor is the opaqueness of Mexican judicial and political institutions especially unusual. If there is a political lesson to be learned by the rest of the world from the Mexican experience, it is that single-party-dominant systems which survive for decades are a breeding ground for collusion and corruption. Japan, India, Italy, Russia, and all other single-party-dominant systems have comparable problems. However, the spectacle of Japanese and Italian prime ministers carrying around suitcases filled with currency never elicited the degree of scorn aroused by Mexico due to the singular mix of condescension and fear with which Americans view their problematic neighbor. Japanese economic might inspired respect, and large, politically active Italian American constituencies restrained members of Congress.

Corruption had long been a feature of Mexico's single-party-dominant political system, where the absence of institutional means of ensuring accountability led to complicitous relations between government authorities, business, and the criminal underworld. Mexico's closed political system led the criminally inclined to believe that their activities would never be questioned. When this was combined with an influx of private money associated with economic reform and an upsurge in drug trafficking money, the result was fatal. What made Mexico different from other such cases was its proximity to the largest market for narcotics consumption in the world, its uncompetitive industrial structure, and its reliance on volatile capital to finance its economic transformation.

The bonds of complicity are being exposed to the light of day for the first time in Mexico. Supporters of the economic reform process have argued that the openness and transparency required by a successful economic reform inevitably create the seeds of political change, challenge vested interests, and reveal the hidden vices of a previously closed system.[1]

A multiple-part challenge has ensued from the latest Mexican crisis. First, the specter of social instability has been raised by the Chiapas uprising and exacerbated by the March 1995 austerity measures imposed to contain the financial crisis. Second, as the old political regime heads toward breakdown, stable electoral democracy is not inevitable, given the dangerous circumstances of polarized elites and the questioned leadership of President Ernesto Zedillo. Third, economic reform and financial stability hang by a hair as political events shake international investors and slow growth. Fourth, the tensile strength of the U.S.-Mexico relationship is tested as a reluctant United

States is compelled to play a supportive role in Mexico's simultaneous political and financial crises. The latest crisis, coming in the wake of the NAFTA ratification battle, has intensified U.S. ambivalence about an ever-deepening involvement with its troubled neighbor.

The reverberations of the Mexican crisis reach far beyond its borders, undermining commitments to open economic policies in other precarious developing economies around the world. Populist forces that seek to delegitimate and reverse market reforms throughout the hemisphere have gotten renewed political mileage from the tarnished moral legitimacy of the three leaders associated with the reform process (Carlos Andres Perez of Venezuela, Fernando Collor de Mello of Brazil, and Carlos Salinas de Gortari of Mexico). Mexico, which serves as a model for much of the hemisphere, now may be the domino that tips the hemisphere in a different direction.

CHIAPAS IN PERSPECTIVE

How is it possible that a guerrilla movement operating out of a territorial base less than one-third the total size of the remote state of Chiapas could turn an entire nation, together with the financial community, on its head. The mountain hideouts of the Zapatista Army of National Liberation (EZLN) are tucked away in the triangle of territory between Ocosingo, Altamirano, and the Guatemalan border. To answer this question is to explain the nature of post-cold war guerrilla activity and to understand the underpinnings of Mexican political culture.

The EZLN is a hard-core Marxist movement, undyingly hostile to the turn to economic orthodoxy initiated in the early 1980s and intensified under Salinas. The ideological motivation of the leadership, in part influenced by the Nicaraguan Sandinista revolution, found NAFTA a natural target for attack. It is a second-generation movement, a direct descendent of the guerrilla movements of the 1970s. Two of the EZLN's leaders, Maria Gloria Benavides Guevara (alias Elisa) and Yanez Muñoz (alias German) adopted a nom de guerre in honor of their murdered siblings, who had died in guerrilla-related incidents in the 1970s. Ironically, the movement's leadership is an ingrown, family affair with tragic personal dimensions, much like the rest of Mexico's political life.

Chiapas was a crisis waiting to happen. It is riven with conflicts between evangelical Christian and Catholic communities, tensions between sedentary farmers and ranchers, racial and ethnic hatreds, the legacy of brutal PRI governors, and a long history of grassroots social activism. Population pressures in the highland Indian communities around San Cristobal de las Casas have forced many into the mountain canyons of southeastern Chiapas and into the Lancondon Forest in search of land. These new communities in no way resemble the more stable, older Indian communities of the highlands. Rather, they are populated by a younger generation socialized without benefit of traditional community values, indoctrinated by social activists, and holding little hope for landownership.

This exodus and the creation of new frontier outposts was fertile soil for the activities of the catechists of Catholic liberation theology. Many villages took names inspired by biblical imagery like New Jerusalem. Bishop Samuel Ruiz is credited with having trained over 2,000 laypersons recruited from the indigenous communities and imbued with the fervor of liberation theology. Special inspiration was found in the book of Exodus and the concept of the promised land. When sedentary indigenous farmers clashed with ranchers over property rights, Bishop Ruiz lectured that the Indians had original rights which justified land invasions. His activist role in land disputes often brought him into the office of the Minister of the Interior in Mexico City. Added to the influence of the church has been the presence of other community organizers, many of whom had been active in the northern states of Mexico in the late 1970s and early 1980s. Still, the impact of the EZLN cannot be explained by the sociology of the region or their military reach.

The EZLN and its charismatic leader, Rafael Sebastian Guillen Vicente (alias Marcos), have the distinction of being the first post-cold war guerrillas. Creatures of the age of the computer and the mass media, their most powerful weapons have been the Internet and the fax machine, not the Uzi or the tank.[2] They have merged the weapons of the post-cold war era with the ideology and disinformation tactics of the cold war years. This may well be the first guerrilla movement ever to calculate the effect of their words and deeds on the stock market. The EZLN's false announcement that they had occupied thirty-eight towns in Chiapas on December 19, 1994, was the immediate prelude to Mexico's December 20 currency devaluation. Their military force was never as significant as their media and psychological cunning. They have convened the world press and marshaled nongovernmental organizations (NGOs) in Europe and the United States with an effectiveness that would make any public relations firm envious.

Everyone from teenagers to middle-class Mexico City matrons swooned over Marcos, who became an overnight media sensation. With his ski mask, his intellectual's irony, and ammunition rounds slung theatrically across his chest as a fashion accessory, *el subcomandante* was the ultimate in chic in a nation of *tapados* (covered ones).[3] His eloquent press communiqués, from "somewhere in the mountains of Chiapas," bent a powerful president to his will, reshaped the national agenda, and accelerated the pace of political democratization. In the best traditions of Mexican surrealism, a murdered candidate and a masked guerrilla dominated the 1994 electoral year. A cult of veneration immediately sprang up around the murdered Colosio in a cynical society where only the dead are pure and worthy of faith.

The Chiapas rebellion and the Colosio murder cracked open the emotional and political life of the nation, revealing a good deal of ambivalence and polarization. The chord that the Zapatistas struck in Mexican society had less to do with support for ideological Marxism than with accumulated discontents that had ripened over the past twenty years. The deprecatory wit and the righteous anger of Marcos resonated in a culture steeped in cynicism, yet longing for a purification of authority, and beset by a crisis of moral and political legitimacy. Because Mexican political authorities were viewed as corrupt, Marcos could be viewed as noble. He reflected the outrage of many common citizens fed up with abuses committed with impunity. The moral resonance of Marcos in Mexican society made Zedillo's efforts to redefine the guerrilla leader as a "delinquent" fall on deaf ears for around half of society.

The vision of a white man (Marcos) leading the Indians stirs complex feelings of guilt and admiration in Mexican society. Mexico's official political culture makes heroes of Indians of the past, but white and mestizo society today lives in a considerably more privileged universe than the Indian. Indians are romanticized in political myth but suffer awful economic and social realities. The hypocrisy and guilt of Mexico's dominant mestizo and white society make it especially susceptible to the eloquent manipulations of Marcos. The guilt is deeply and historically rooted. During the conquest of Mexico, the Aztecs mistook Cortés for Quetzalcoatl, a blue-eyed god that legend foretold would come from the sea to redeem the Aztecs. Cortés was, of course, a cruel conqueror. Marcos expiates the sin of the conquistador and redeems the white man. His mystique merges with Christian theology and traditions of martyrdom. Marcos' press communiqués, which often refer to his own death, subliminally suggest a Christlike crucifixion to redeem the sins of society and to defend the Indian meek. At the same time, Chiapas arouses a fear that this "other," Indian Mexicc could rise and engulf the nation's middle and upper classes.

The carefully cultivated image of the masked Zapatista was a master stroke of cultural metaphor. The mask embodies Mexico's wary attitude toward the outside world, an attitude that is rooted in the Conquest and traditional Indian maskmaking practices that survive to this day. Modern Mexico retains a fetishistic fascination with masks, deception, and maintaining a hidden, protected self. Mexico is a wounded nation, and the mask is both a defense mechanism and the route to self revelation.[4] Before Marcos, the Mexican popular imagination was captured by Santos, the masked wrestler who fought evil and defended the poor. More recently, the masked wrestler Superbarrio has run in the same traditions, acting as a political prop in tandem with the Asamblea de Barrios, a radicalized organization defending tenants' rights in Mexico City. Clearly, Zedillo removed Marcos' ski mask in hope that the real Marcos would be a disappointment compared with the mythical Marcos constructed in the imagination.

Finally, Mexico is a nation born of revolution and has a ready-made sympathy learned in grade school for revolutionary heroes. The EZLN was virtually guaranteed some degree of popular sympathy when they adopted the figure of the agrarian revolutionary hero Emiliano Zapata, even though Zapata never had a presence in the state of Chiapas. In doing so, the guerrillas both appropriated a national myth and launched a cunning attack on the psyche of Salinas, an individual who named everything, from the presidential helicopter to his son, after Zapata. Salinas had devoted his undergraduate and graduate studies to rural issues and was, therefore, pained at being politically outflanked on agrarian issues. A member of the 1960s generation, he would be especially reluctant to bloody his hands with a tough response to the uprising.

Some likened the Chiapas incident to a wake-up call to attend to the nation's poor, and a collective attack of conscience is sweeping all levels of Mexican society. The debate on the social costs of economic reform is also driven by the fatigue of six years of real wage declines from 1982 to 1988 and the slow real wage increases from 1988 to 1994. The social policy preoccupation reflects a broad, hemisphere-wide concern with decrepit health and educational services, rural poverty, rampant urban growth, and declining social conditions. Social needs are real and urgent, but the danger of the latest rediscovery of poverty is that it degenerates into expedient demagoguery designed to undermine support for market-based economic policies. Ironically, Chiapas occurred on the watch of the first Mexican president in many years to devote resources to social issues. Social spending increased dramatically from 1988 to 1993, with over 50 percent of the federal budget devoted to social spending.

Salinista policymakers never deluded themselves into believing that Mexico was on the verge of turning into a first world nation, although they delighted in letting the foreign media and investors believe the myth. They knew that Mexico has always been a nation of deep contradictions, existing simultaneously in the twenty-first and the nineteenth centuries. Incomes would not rise dramatically anytime soon. Marcos alluded to these social contrasts when he said in one of his many interviews, "There is a guerrilla law with respect to the velocity of a guerrilla column. It says that the velocity of the column is only as fast as the slowest man. This nation should be the same. How fast should its economy advance? As rapidly as its poorest state. One part of the country cannot be in the First World while the other, our world in Chiapas, is annihilated."[5] But policymakers cannot permit the progress of the rest of Mexico to be held hostage to the progress of Chiapas.

The financial collapse of 1995 has renewed the tension between the painful discipline of macroeconomic stability (which requires austerity) and the exigencies of poverty. The renewed need to restrain wages to contain the inflationary impact of a massive devaluation falls upon a population already weary of austerity. The risk faced by Ernesto Zedillo is that of a Chiapas-inspired contagion effect of social instability that spreads to the labor unions and the cities. And while the EZLN appears to be greatly weakened, its web of safe houses in Veracruz and the state of Mexico makes it impossible to rule out the existence of cell groups in other states like Oaxaca, Durango, or Puebla.

POLITICAL LIBERALIZATION AND THE EXTRA-CONSTITUTIONAL TEMPTATION

Mexico is living through a refounding of its political order at a moment when the bonds of civilized conduct are weak. Mexico's crisis has been aggravated by the deterioration of self-restraint in elite civic culture. Assassination, kidnapping, and guerrilla violence violate powerful norms and cannot be explained in narrow forensic terms. People act out their violent dreams and interests in the political arena more readily when the political culture at large has been poisoned. For the first time in post-revolutionary history, the fundamental stability and social fabric of Mexico are under serious pressure.

Was the seed of violence planted years ago when obstinate single-party proclivities were unwilling to abide by a peaceful verdict delivered at the polling booth? Decades of playing fast and loose with electoral results have undermined respect for the rule of law. The harvest of official intolerance has been bitter opposition party hatred, itself a danger to the refounding of Mexico. Did the PRI's conversion to the cause of electoral purity come too late to save the country from descending into polarization and extralegal temptations? President Salinas' resort to interim governorships to solve local electoral disputes and rid the regime of burdensome governors set dangerous precedents for fiddling with the constitutional order.

Opposition parties also bear responsibility for degrading Mexico's political ethics by flirting with destabilizing tactics and indulging in dishonest portrayals of their own political strength. The encouragement of postelectoral demonstrations by opposition parties carries an implicit message of blackmail—cede the election or there will be violence in the streets. Or did the erosion of Mexico's political culture occur when mothers attending peace rallies for Chiapas permitted their children to don ski masks in imitation of the Zapatistas? In chic circles, violence is considered comprehensible if the cause is just. Was a Zapatista gun pointed at the nation's head in the name of free elections and social justice less evil than the one pointed at Colosio's head?

The August 1994 presidential elections were unique because, for the first time, important elements of Mexican political life attempted to precipitate a crisis of governability that could have resulted in either a pacted transition, an interim presidency, a power-sharing government of national unity, or even a military solution. Ideas were circulated widely in the press and the intellectual community that belittled the electoral process as insufficiently reliable and viewed the installation of a negotiated coalition government as a desirable outcome. The poison seed of extralegal pressure tactics and an alteration of the constitutional order was planted and legitimated by some of the most distinguished voices in Mexican elite circles.

Active precedents occurred in the 1991 gubernatorial elections in San Luis Potosi and Guanajuato, where postelectoral demonstrations and international pressure forced government authorities into a "second round" of brokered political solutions.[6] In fact, the inspiration for the idea sprang from the ideological and political clash between Cuauhtemoc Cardenas and Carlos Salinas in the disputed 1988 presidential elections. For some, the 1994 race was to be a replay of the 1988 confrontation, a "train wreck" between the Right and the Left, which could be mediated only by third parties and a coalition government. The prospect of 150,000 demonstrators in front of the National Palace after the elections was especially worrisome, given the newly violent atmosphere of Mexico.

The idea of an interim presidency was in vogue, promoted by some in a genuine effort to avert a feared pre-civil war situation. Others may have promoted the idea in a more opportunistic effort to change the balance of power via negotiation rather than the electoral process.[7] The concept of a grand coalition resonated to portions of the Mexican elite that, even unconsciously, may have yearned to piece together the all-inclusive, revolutionary umbrella party of Calles. Unlike democracy, with its cruel law of winners and losers, the grand 1929 pact of Calles, which originated the PRI, offered a niche to all players. In a political system where the Left was increasingly marginalized and unable to construct a winning electoral coalition, the rejuggling of the grand coalition within an interim PRI government did not look so bad.

The problem with the concept is that it has introduced the notion that the constitutional order can be altered for some greater good or for political expediency. Reducing popular rejection of extralegal political negotiation solutions undermines institution-building at a time when Mexico is attempting to consolidate the rule of law. More dangerously, once the concept has been legitimated, any political force that has an interest in making a power grab can avail itself of the notion.

The Party of the Democratic Revolution (PRD) was the vehicle of choice for those who either sympathized with the EZLN or favored the use of radicalized tactics to overturn the PRI—with or without the electoral process. An overt battle between the PRD's moderate and radical wings erupted over the party's relationship to the EZLN, with hard-liners preferring destabilization to electoral politics. The Cardenistas were rightly skeptical regarding the possibility of a fair election, but Cuauhtemoc Cardenas did little to discourage his supporters' belief that the only credible election would be one in which the PRD won national power. Electoral legitimacy was defined not by the fairness of the process but by the outcome. It was far from clear that Cardenas, like the PRI itself, was prepared to accept a free election that did not result in his victory. Creating instability in order to negotiate positions in an interim or power-sharing form of government is more appropriate to nations mired in civil war than to nations embarked on a democratic transition. Ultimately, the heat was also on the PRD, to abandon the objective of destroying its adversary and embrace the goal of forging fair rules of the electoral game.

The U.S. government stepped in to stabilize what it perceived to be dangerous postelectoral scenarios by supporting election observation via the channeling of financial resources and moral support through the National Endowment for Democracy (NED), the National Democratic Institute (NDI), and the U.S. Agency for International Development (USAID). The NDI directly financed a major, national effort of Mexican NGOs to mount a quick count and a poll-watching effort the day of the election, and sought informational exchanges with the Mexican Federal Electoral Institute, the entity responsible for administering elections. Official support for NGO activism was a thinly veiled substitute for direct U.S. governmental involvement. The policy ran into some glitches when it was recognized that NDI support for NGOs could backfire and turn into a potentially disruptive force in the 1994 elections. Policymakers in Washington and Mexico City cast about for an external force to discipline NGO passions.

That external force was found in the United Nations, which ended up monitoring and disciplining the Mexican NGO monitors, and professionalizing Mexican NGO activities and statistical methodologies to encourage greater impartiality.[8]

The off-loading of democratization policy to the NGO community had thorny implications. The Clinton administration was divided about the advisability of relying so heavily on NGOs. Many NGOs do courageous and valuable work in the arena of human rights, the environment, and emergency relief. Realistically, however, not all NGOs are disinterested players, and a very fine line separates many NGOs from outright partisan advocacy. NGO activity is surrounded by a halo of democratic legitimacy and impartiality, but Mexico is a far cry from the Tocquevillean ideal of civil society. Many within the NGO community of election monitors felt that election fraud was inevitable and that the recognition of a PRI victory would constitute, a priori, the legitimation of fraud. Official support for NGOs, therefore, left the United States in an ambiguous position with regard to exercising partisan influence in Mexican elections. The NGO falls into a gray zone in today's more murky definitions of sovereignty and intervention.

In this troubled context, the upcoming August 21, 1994, presidential elections acquired a moral dimension that transcended mere politics. Average Mexicans sensed that rejuvenation could emanate from a clean election, which would reaffirm their vocation as a civilized people and provide a moral catharsis for the nation. In this respect, the average Mexican showed greater wisdom and maturity than many of the most esteemed voices of the cultural elite. Ultimately, the danger of postelectoral destabilization receded because very few doubted that the election was clean. And NAFTA functioned exactly as its supporters predicted. It mobilized international attention so as to reduce Mexico's single-party-dominant regime's margin for self-preservation outside of clean elections.

Mexico may achieve democracy, but its fledgling democracy still faces considerable risk. The absence of a solid consensus on the parameters of economic policy remains a worrisome obstacle to a smooth democratic transition. Mexican democratization will not be complete until a party of the Left is formed that is compatible with the basic commonsense outlines of a market economy.[9] The Mexican Left has yet to fully appreciate the lessons of democratization in

Chile, where consensus on economic reform made for a stable political opening. Unfortunately, some still wish to vindicate the statist strands of Mexico's revolutionary tradition and to prove that the socialist dream did not die with the death of the Soviet Union. This raises a corollary problem—the radicalization of the Mexican Left condemns it to a small-party, minority status. Yet if the Left is unable to come to power via peaceful electoral means, its commitment to electoral democracy may fade further.

It is becoming ever more difficult to convince the Mexican political community to coalesce around a set of shared goals. Fragmentation, polarization, and mutual suspicions are rife within the PRI and between political parties over everything from Chiapas to economic policy. This dearth of consensus, with origins in the controversies prompted by the orthodox, conservative economic policies of President Miguel de la Madrid (1982-88), has grown noisier in recent years. The rupture of consensus deepened under Salinas, whose radical economic reforms represented a departure from the historic precepts and legacy of the Mexican Revolution. This bitter debate over economic paradigms has been exacerbated by the collapse of the peso. Virtually every constituent interest group within and without the PRI is discontented. Zedillo's natural allies within the business community have been alienated by an economic stabilization plan that imposes high interest rates and taxes. Labor resents the real wage reductions of the austerity program. Electoral reform pits hard-liners and populists in the PRI against Zedillo's reform inclinations. The press and electronic media have achieved almost total freedom and, as a result, increasingly reflect these strident differences and complicate Zedillo's efforts to get his message out. Zedillo seems torn in contradictory directions as he struggles to build consensus, exposing himself to charges of policy zigzags.

The task of building democracy and consensus is further complicated because Zedillo labors under a debilitating national debate over his own competence and over whether he is a weak or a strong president. The bumpy management of the devaluation and the resignation of Treasury Secretary Jaime Serra within thirty days after the inauguration raised doubts about the technical abilities of the economic team. Zedillo's deliberate abdication of an activist leadership role in the PRI and his acceptance of a more independent role for Congress led many to assume that he was a weak president.

Mexicans accustomed to an Aztec presidency had difficulty distinguishing between the limitations on presidential power found in a democracy and weak leadership. Zedillo's dramatic conflict with Carlos Salinas and his aggressive program to fight drug traffickers and build a true judicial system may ultimately be the foundations on which his popularity and presidency rest. The extra-constitutional temptations that surfaced during the August 1994 presidential election could emerge at a later date, however, if the perception of a leadership vacuum persists for a prolonged period.

The extra-constitutional temptation can be restrained if Mexicans content themselves with expressing their wishes through the electoral process. Zedillo has three years to recover from the economic crisis before midterm elections offer voters the opportunity to issue a political judgment at the federal level. But the Mexican electoral calendar is filled with opportunities at the state and local levels. The devaluations of the 1980s sparked a cycle of political discontent that led Mexicans to vote for opposition parties in large numbers, first in state and local elections. The gubernatorial races of 1995 offer the PAN a good opportunity to capitalize on the protest vote. This was seen in the February 1995 elections in the large industrial state of Jalisco, where the PAN swept the local Congress, major municipalities, and the governorship. The crisis offers Zedillo a historic opportunity to define himself as the first president to bring completely fair elections and judicial transparency to Mexico.

THE FINANCIAL CRACK

What has come to be known as the Christmas devaluation was not a complete surprise. The peso was under pressure throughout 1994 as national elections took place under a cloud of assassinations and guerrilla movements, the trade deficit grew, and rumors of a devaluation seeped out from the Zedillo campaign as early as April 1994. International competition for capital also moved money out of Mexico with the rise in U.S. interest rates and the shift of speculative capital to Brazil and other emerging markets.

Some economists had argued as early as 1993 that devaluation was inevitable. Former President Salinas and former Treasury Secretary Pedro Aspe, they claimed, had based their anti-inflation strategy on an overvalued peso. As a result, the overvalued currency stifled Mexican exports and encouraged imports as the trade deficit and current account deficit ballooned. A flood of U.S. exports took Mexico's trade deficit to around 8 percent of GDP. The Achilles' heel of Mexico's trade deficit was excessive reliance on speculative capital to finance the deficit. Mexico's net foreign investment was heavily weighted toward volatile capital, with 75-80 percent in securities and 15-20 percent in direct fixed investment.[10]

Many portfolio investors in Mexican securities say they felt deceived by the devaluation. No government gives prior notice of a devaluation, but Zedillo and Serra had loudly proclaimed their commitment to the peso. Investors had wagered on the confidence inherited from Salinas and felt that the new government breached an implicit contract. Some investors on Wall Street argued that large trade deficits are necessary to developing economies and do not inevitably require the devaluation of a currency. Some analysts suggested that investors would have remained in the Mexican market had an iron-clad commitment to the peso been made early on. These observers prescribed a restrictive monetary policy to reduce the supply of pesos through the sale of bonds or other assets and the adoption of an Argentine-style currency board to peg the peso to the dollar.

The handling of the devaluation made matters worse, eroding confidence in the new government. The fluid communications previously maintained by Treasury officials and Wall Street slowed to a halt. Press conferences were scheduled and suddenly canceled. The announcement of the macroeconomic policy measures that normally accompany a devaluation came more than a week after the devaluation, and only after delays and the leakage of documents. A full-blown crisis of confidence was the result.

Regardless of the many virtues of the economic and financial framework put in place during the twelve years of reform under Miguel de la Madrid and Carlos Salinas, the economic model contained enough inherent vulnerabilities to make it unable to resist the political shocks of 1994. The dream of a top-down, gradual reform process, in which economic reform preceded political opening, proved illusory and flawed. Economic reform undid Mexico's traditional political arrangements, which in turn undermined the confidence of foreign investors who struggled to understand the Byzantine movements of Mexico's political breakdown.

Inflation reduction will take precedence in the aftermath. Labor discipline and a new round of wage restraint will be hard to attain, and may be achieved only at the expense of labor's historic political alliance with the PRI. There is a trade-off between economic austerity and the PRI's political support. Wall Street investors demanding fiscal responsibility should be prepared to see an erosion in the PRI's electoral strength and the acceleration of the democratization process.

Mexican labor suffers from adjustment fatigue after six years of real wage declines (1982-88) and six years of slow recovery (1988-94). Discipline used to be guaranteed by a pliant, corporatist union leadership, but another round of belt-tightening may strengthen the hand of young malcontents. The Salinas years deemphasized pattern contracts and encouraged decentralized wage negotiations to reflect plant-level productivity. Market economics and decentralization imply some loss of control over wages and union politics. The pillar of Mexican anti-inflation policy was the *pacto* signed in October 1994, which continued the wage and price negotiations institutionalized in 1987 under President Miguel de la Madrid and continued under Salinas. The *pacto* was abandoned in the aftermath of the Zedillo devaluation. The demise of the *pacto* is yet another symptom of the difficulty of achieving consensus in the post-Salinas era and erosion of the discipline imposed by the persuasive power of a strong state.

Mexico's strategic insertion into the North American and European markets had one immediate benefit. Although the White House was initially slow to appreciate the severity of the Mexican crisis, Washington did galvanize unprecedented lines of credit in the sum of $18 billion from the United States, Canada, the Bank for International Settlements (BIS), and a consortium of more than ten commercial banks. But even bolder measures were needed to halt the market's slide and to prevent a domino effect in emerging markets around the world. The Clinton administration decided that it would be easier to fix a short-term liquidity crisis in Mexico than to try to fix a bigger mess later, after it had affected financial markets throughout the world. When it became clear that the initial $18 billion package was insufficient to shore up confidence, the Clinton administration announced its intention to offer a $40 billion loan guarantee program. Anti-NAFTA forces immediately began to rally against the package. They were joined by many of the Republican freshmen congressmen, some of whom were inspired by the fire-breathing, Wall Street versus

Main Street populism of Pat Buchanan. Others were swayed by a neomonetarist vision—promoted by Jude Wanninski, Jack Kemp, Larry Kudlow, and others—to the effect that the Mexican peso could be revalued to around 3.5 pesos to the dollar.[11]

Clinton chose to bypass Congress and by executive order authorized the use of $20 billion in exchange stabilization funds (ESF). Washington mobilized an additional $17.8 billion in International Monetary Fund (IMF) supports, $10 billion from the BIS, and $1 billion contributed by several Latin American countries. The plan requires Mexico to pass its oil export receipts through the U.S. Federal Reserve Bank of New York before reaching Mexico so that they would be available to the United States in the event of a default. This measure, together with the adoption of high interest rates, monetary restraint, and fiscal cuts, led to no small measure of resentment against Washington. The price of the package was high, both in Mexico and in Washington.

The Washington financial support package has left no small political storm in its wake. Zedillo's perceived unwillingness to stand up to Washington was strongly questioned in Mexico. Clinton's bold commitment to Mexico may be good policy, but it rests on a fragile political base. His end run of Congress earned enemies. Most worrisome, the general perception that the United States has become involved in a financial Vietnam in a country of questionable moral repute has weakened U.S. appetite for foreign engagement across the board. The apparent contagion between the Mexican peso crisis and the abrupt March slide of the U.S. dollar led those with doubts about the wisdom of NAFTA to revisit the question of economic integration with Mexico. The repercussions are likely to be felt for years on both sides of the border.

Mexico has lost hope of achieving investment-grade status from the rating agencies and will no longer proceed toward the next phase of attracting a new group of conservative portfolio investors in the pension and insurance industries. The mix of foreign investment in portfolio investment versus direct investment will now tip in favor of the latter, as the logic of NAFTA continues to attract fixed investment. One of the most important features of the restructuring that has occurred since 1982 is the integration of Mexican and U.S. industrial production. Most of Mexico's exports to the United States are finished manufactured goods and intra-industry semi-finished goods rather than oil. Capital investment is long-term in nature, and is not as sensitive to short-term currency fluctuations as are financial securities. Mexico's insertion into global trading arrangements will ultimately bring benefits. Direct fixed investment as a result of NAFTA is likely to provide a structural underpinning to Mexico's manufactured exports in the years ahead.

Ultimately, the Mexican crisis is as much about new trends in global capital markets as it is about Mexico. The overwhelming volume of capital that was poured into emerging markets by mutual fund investors was more volatile and less informed than the ponderous, but more enduring, investment decisions made by direct foreign investors. Moreover, the quantities of dollar investments from Wall Street far outweighed the historic presence of international financial institutions (IFI), limiting the influence of the IFIs on market dynamics. The "flight to quality" that occurred after the Mexican market's collapse also reflects the fact that the interest rate decisions of the U.S. Federal Reserve and the German Bundesbank probably have more impact on capital flows in and out of emerging markets than do good Mexican fiscal and monetary policies. Finally, the indiscriminatory "tequila effect" of the Mexican market on emerging markets around the world says as much about the decision dynamics of panic as it says about Mexico's inherent economic prospects.[12]

THE ORDERING AND DISORDERING OF BILATERAL RELATIONS

The Bush and Salinas governments were a high-water mark in U.S.-Mexican relations. Both men entered office with an exhilarating sense of paradigm-shattering, historic opportunity to bury the hatchet of ancestral enmity. They were pledged to developing a new consensus revolving around faith in market economics, open trading systems, and mutual respect. The open economic orientation of both nations was nudged forward by a singular moment in world events. The collapse of messianic Marxism and global convergence regarding market economics made reconciliation between the United States and Mexico easier. Bush and Salinas shared an internationalist philosophy, and both publics were willing to make a leap of faith together with their leaders. The period of Bush/Salinas intergovernmental felicity was named the "Spirit of Houston," after the first meeting between the two newly elected presidents.

But events since January 1, 1994, have contributed to a profound reordering, and potential disordering, of bilateral relations. The free-trade agreement that was conceived in the summer of political romance in June 1989 was born in a winter of wariness by November 1993. How durable is the Spirit of Houston in the aftermath of Chiapas and the Christmas devaluation?

Although trade and capital markets are increasingly global, the political pressures building at the grassroots level in both the United States and Mexico are increasingly inward-looking. A backlash against open economic policies has been building in both countries since the early 1990s. Indeed, the U.S. domestic consensus behind NAFTA was tenuous from the beginning. In spite of the efforts of the Clinton administration to keep the momentum positive, the ugly battle to pass NAFTA in the U.S. Congress in November 1993 left one Mexican official muttering, "We may pass NAFTA, but we will end up hating one another." The voice of Ross Perot epitomized the new, insular spirit that would soon animate a large portion of U.S. political opinion. The United States had turned into Mexico's worst nightmare—an irascible, perpetually demanding entity issuing an escalating and ever more intrusive series of demands (labor and environmental demands from Democrats, and monetary and investment policy demands from Republicans).

The U.S. receptiveness to involvement with Mexico has grown more and more ambivalent as Mexico's need for support has grown exponentially. The Mexican financial crisis may have been the straw that broke the camel's back and greatly diminished overall U.S. interest in foreign engagement. The Clinton administration's proposal to offer loan guarantees to Mexico in February 1995 met with a dismal end in the U.S. Congress. The subsequent controversy over the use of ESF to stabilize the Mexican peso indicated that U.S. tolerance for shouldering foreign burdens had shrunk.

It may be useful to recover elements that, during the brief interlude of the Spirit of Houston, smoothed bilateral relations. The success of the Spirit of Houston relied on a four-part implicit bargain. The first and truly revolutionary factor reshaping bilateral relations was Mexico's redefinition of its own intense brand of nationalism. Mexico let down its guard and entertained the notion that perhaps the United

States was not inevitably an enemy that would destroy its national sovereignty. This was no small leap of faith, given that mistrust of the United States had long been an article of faith on which all Mexicans could agree. Mexico acknowledged that its closed economy, maintained in the name of sovereignty and nationalism, offered illusory autarky. The choice is not between dependency and independence, but how best to manage an inevitable interdependence.

The second factor reshaping bilateral relations was the Bush administration's conscientious effort to avoid anything that could be interpreted as untoward meddling, acutely aware that the Mexican government had taken a political risk in moving closer to the United States. It was understood that Mexico had retooled its nationalist doctrines, not to invite U.S. intervention in its domestic affairs but with the intention of capturing larger foreign investment flows. NAFTA was conceived by Bush as a strictly commercial agreement rather than a European Community-style initiative. Bush also followed a hands-off approach toward Mexican politics. The gradualism of the Bush approach assumed that NAFTA and a successful economic reform would bring greater democracy, environmental purity, and higher wages in Mexico. The opposition gubernatorial victories in Baja California in 1989 and Chihuahua in 1992 suggested that Mexico was already on a trajectory toward political liberalization.

The third prerequisite for the containment of conflict was the deliberate delinkage of contentious issues, combined with the institutionalization of government-to-government communication. During the Reagan/de la Madrid years, tensions over narcotics or Central American foreign policy became "the tail that wagged the dog," as one U.S. State Department official described it. Tension in one area of bilateral relations prevented forward movement in other areas of the bilateral agenda. The Bush/Salinas years were characterized by a deliberate effort to create multiple, parallel issue tracks, preventing the paralysis of the relationship due to the spillover of conflicts. Annual Binational Commission meetings between the two heads of state and their cabinets became effective vehicles for processing bilateral demands. The machinery was reinforced by Bush and Salinas' hands-on leadership.

Fourth and finally, the new relationship based on NAFTA assumed a degree of fundamental consensus in both nations regarding the parameters of economic policy. The United States assumed that

Mexico's economic reforms were relatively stable and enjoyed significant support at home. Similarly, Mexico assumed that the United States would continue its commitment to leading the global forces of free trade, as it has done since Bretton Woods.

The conditions that made the Spirit of Houston possible have been shaken badly in the post-NAFTA era. The Clinton administration did not have the luxury of dealing with a strong or stable Mexican government, which led to a strong temptation to intervene in its internal politics. The U.S. impulse to meddle was difficult to resist, especially given that the Democratic Party foreign policy style is rooted in the missionary tradition of Wilsonian idealism and places the promotion of democracy as a central goal of American foreign policy. Mexico is tough terrain for the exercise of Wilsonian dreams. There are no white hats and black hats. The Clinton administration tried to balance its desire to speed Mexican democratization, its wish to avoid provoking a nationalistic backlash, the U.S. interest in seeing economic reform succeed, and a national security concern for the stability of Mexico. Latin America policy hands who cut their teeth during the dark days of authoritarian rule in the hemisphere mistook Mexico for El Salvador or Chile. The Clinton administration's activism during the 1994 presidential election has introduced new precedents and a new element of suspicion into government-to-government relations.

Mexicans also are sending a mixed message regarding the desirability of U.S. intervention for the first time. For most of the twentieth century, Mexicans disdained both the "bad" realpolitik interventionism of Republicans and the "good" high-minded interventionism of Democrats. Woodrow Wilson's well-intentioned bombardment of the port of Veracruz against the dictator Huerta was scorned by the Mexican revolutionary Carranza. But the redefinition of Mexican nationalism that occurred with the passage of NAFTA has loosened taboos regarding political sovereignty. Today, Mexico's democratizers do not universally reject external pressures, and some actively seek to inject the weight of the United States to alter the domestic political balance in Mexico.

The U.S. Congress and media have become the object of efforts by Mexican intellectuals and NGOs who are discontented with their nation's incomplete democratization and who disagree with economic reform and trade integration policies. The U.S. NAFTA vote created leverage that Mexican opponents of economic reform could use to boost their voice and internationalize their conflicts. Implicit alliances between opponents of market reforms in Mexico and the forces of trade protection in the United States now spill across the border into the congressional hearing rooms of Washington. More worrisome, some Mexicans may be tempted to take destabilizing actions to attract media and congressional attention. The international community rewards spectacular and explosive political acts with its attention. The deliberate manufacture of incidents for the benefit of television is a part of the Mexican political repertoire. Interestingly, the EZLN forbade the Mexican television network, Televisa, to cover the peace accords on the grounds that the network was biased, but did welcome CNN.

The preeminence of federal government-to-government relations and the strong presidential leadership styles of Bush and Salinas have been overtaken by new channels of communication and pressure. The ability of the two executive branches to set the bilateral agenda and contain conflicts has been diminished. U.S. congressional activism is on the rise and is one unanticipated by-product of the NAFTA ratification process. Members of Congress have no incentive to manage conflict since they do not face, as do federal agencies, the need to negotiate with Mexican counterparts to search for practical solutions to daily problems. Some congressmen engage in Mexico-bashing to score cost-free political points in their home districts. The fierce congressional opposition to NAFTA has created a quasi-permanent corps of hostile congressmen who, in the absence of strong presidential leadership, may increasingly drive the agenda.

The practical effect of the increasing integration of the two societies and NGO activism may well be increased democratization at the cost of decreased governability and increased conflict. Conflict management in government-to-government relations has also been complicated by the ability of NGOs and the media to set the issue agenda. The elevation of society-to-society relations as a deliberate policy objective weakens executive branch capabilities and accelerates the emergence of a North American market in political ideas, cross-border lobbying, and a new style of North American political entrepreneur and internationalized NGO.

A related tension has been the Clinton administration's interest in achieving innovative policy linkages between trade and social policy.

By definition, this undermines the principle and practice of delinking issues in order to contain conflict. It may be intellectually gratifying to observe that the world is a global mesh of interrelationships, but practicality suggests that problems are better solved discretely. The NAFTA "side agreements" creating dispute resolution mechanisms for environmental and labor issues could increase trade-related litigation. The U.S.-Canadian free-trade experience suggests that dispute resolution can backfire politically by attracting attention to disputes, creating new resentments and headlines. Most important, the principle of linking economic relations to a vast array of social issues has been enshrined.

The first challenge facing U.S. policymakers is to prevent the erosion of governability in North American relationships. Conflict has been amplified as U.S.-Mexican relations are propelled into the three-ring circus of the U.S. Congress, Wall Street, and the media. The new NAFTA dispute resolution institutions may invite dispute as much as they resolve it. The ability of nascent North American institutions and government-to-government relations to process demands and manage conflict may well be inundated by the forces of a new trinational civil society.

Relations between the Mexican and U.S. presidencies are smooth, but the weight of Congress, financial markets, state governments, NGOs, and the media exceeds presidential power. A mirror image is developing in Mexico, where absolute presidential authority is giving way to more pluralism. The power of the presidency and governments around the globe contend with trends toward plebiscitary democracy, interactive media, and pressure group politics. In sum, bilateral relations increasingly are defined by forces outside the executive branch. Both societies may find it increasingly difficult to generate consensus in both bilateral and domestic affairs. The strong voice of American leadership is necessary to prevent a slide toward destructive quarrelsomeness.

The second danger is the introduction of new forms of U.S. intervention at the same time that the traditional taboos of Mexican nationalism have been weakened, blurring the boundaries of sovereign decision-making. Washington unwittingly may be courting an anti-American backlash in Mexico. U.S. policy must resist the temptation of moralistic preaching, avoid being used by Mexican domestic forces, provide support for democratization without influencing political outcomes or inadvertently destabilizing Mexico, and refrain from imposing costly first world standards on struggling third world economies.

The third danger facing U.S. policy is how to prevent a reversal of economic reform in Mexico and the hemisphere at large. Economic reform reversal is a distinct possibility in some countries in the hemisphere, as the election of Rafael Caldera in Venezuela demonstrates. NAFTA raised expectations in Mexico that it would quickly stimulate growth and large volumes of foreign investment. Support for economic reform could be endangered if there is a failure to achieve the original goals of generating economic growth within a reasonable time.[13] The first four years of the Salinas administration saw a steady pickup in growth and investment, stepped-up social spending, and low inflation. The momentum was interrupted by the uncertainty leading up to NAFTA ratification and by Mexico's determination to achieve single-digit inflation. Growth slowed in 1992, came to a standstill by 1993, and plunged into a severe recession after the 1994 devaluation. It is critical that the United States do everything in its power to encourage the return to economic growth in Mexico.

In sum, relations among the nations of North America have entered a new and more treacherous phase. The NAFTA has unleashed unforeseen political dynamics in the U.S body politic at the same time that the newly unpredictable situation in Mexico generates unprecedented new demands on U.S. policy capabilities. Containment of the Mexican financial crisis is essential, not only because of the national security implications for the United States but also because of the ripple effects that an ongoing crisis would have in global financial markets and in the hemisphere.

The promise originally held by NAFTA and the Mexican economic reform need not be in vain when the long view of events is taken. The financial crisis has not undone the achievements of structural reform implemented during the Salinas administration, and with the restoration of a stable currency, Mexico may emerge stronger and wiser, as did Chile after its banking and currency crisis of the 1980s. If the Zedillo administration is able to restore political confidence on the basis of a thoroughgoing judicial reform and fair elections, his presidency could well be remembered as the one that brought complete democratization and moral renovation to Mexico.

NOTES

1. M. Delal Baer and Sidney Weintraub, "The Interplay Between Economic and Political Opening: The Sequence in Mexico," *Washington Quarterly* 15, 2 (Spring 1992).

2. See, for instance, Tod Robberson, "Mexican Rebels Using a High-Tech Weapon: Internet Helps Rally Support," *Washington Post*, February 20, 1995, p. A21, col. 1.

3. The potential PRI candidates for the presidency are called *tapados* (covered ones). They are referred to as *tapados* because their candidacies are officially undeclared and because the victor is hidden in the mind of the incumbent president, who ultimately makes the decision. Many Mexicans delight in the game of trying to peer behind the veil of secrecy and guess who will be the candidate, but Zedillo is unlikely to have either the desire or the ability to select his candidate in this time-honored fashion.

4. Nobel laureate Octavio Paz, in his classic work *The Labryinth of Solitude*, places special emphasis on the metaphor of the mask.

5. *Proceso* no. 903 (February 21, 1994): 15.

6. M. Delal Baer, *The 1991 Mexican Midterm Elections* (Washington, D.C.: Center for Strategic and International Studies, 1991).

7. Jorge Castañeda, "Vias de transicion," *Proceso* no. 917 (May 30, 1994): 44-46, and "Un programa comun," *Proceso* no. 919 (June 13, 1994): 38-42; Gerardo Albarran de Alba, "La crisis de credibilidad envuelve las elecciones; alto riesgo de que el pais se torne ingovernable," *Proceso* no. 920 (June 20, 1994): 10-13 (interview with Jorge Castañeda regarding the Grupo San Angel).

8. M. Delal Baer, "Observing the Mexican Election Observers," *Wall Street Journal*, June 3, 1994, "The Americas" section.

9. M. Delal Baer, "Mexico's Election: Forward Leap," *Journal of Commerce*, August 26, 1994, "Editorial/Opinion" section.

10. M. Delal Baer, "Mexico: Politics and the Peso in Transition," *Global Business White Paper* no. 15 (New York: The Conference Board, 1995).

11. Patrick Buchanan, "U.S. Taxpayers Could Pay for Mexican Bailout," *Houston Chronicle*, January 17, 1995, 2 Star Edition, p. 19, "Bailout Stampede," *Washington Times*, January 25, 1995, and "Mexico and the GOP," *Washington Times*, January 25, 1995; Lawrence Kudlow, "Mexico," *National Review* (January 19, 1995); David Malpass, "The Mexican Peso: 3.5 or Bust," *Wall Street Journal*, January 11, 1995, p. A-14.

12. Moises Naim, "Mexico's Un-Mexican Story," *Foreign Policy* 99 (Spring 1995): 112-130.

13. My thanks to Jesus Reyes Heroles, of the Grupo de Economistas y Asociados (GEA) in Mexico City, whose helpful comments during a panel

discussion at the Centro de Investigacion y Docencia Economica (CIDE) on February 14-15, 1994, assisted the development of my thinking on this point.

2

The FTA and NAFTA: One Canadian's Perspective

A. Edward Safarian

This chapter looks retrospectively at the development and short-term effects of the Canada-United States Free Trade Agreement (FTA), and prospectively at the North American Free Trade Agreement (NAFTA). The emphasis will be on the government of Canada's reasons for participating in these treaties and on some of the economic and political problems which have arisen from them. While the FTA can be considered to have had positive economic effects over time, both its substance and the way in which it was implemented created serious political strains in Canada. There were important lessons here for the subsequent debate in the United States on the NAFTA. What follows is one Canadian's viewpoint, but an attempt is made to present, in broad terms, the consensus—or lack thereof—on these issues.

WHY THE CANADIAN GOVERNMENT PROPOSED THE FTA

Canadian political initiatives for freer trade with the United States go back to the middle of the nineteenth century. The present initiative began in 1983 with the publication of two studies by External Affairs Canada, the government ministry responsible for trade, proposing that free trade be considered in certain sectors. This initiative, it may be noted, was under a Liberal government headed by Prime Minister Pierre Trudeau. It was in part a response to the 1979 U.S. Trade Agreement Act and President Ronald Reagan's declared intention to pursue hemispheric trade agreements. A joint study program of the two governments, early in 1984, soon made it clear that the United States found a managed sectoral approach unacceptable.

The Conservative government, elected in the fall of 1984, began new efforts in cooperation with the United States to determine how to enhance trade. In September 1985, the chairman and most of the members of a federal Royal Commission indicated that they supported discussions on bilateral free trade. A few weeks later, the Prime Minister announced his government's interest in a bilateral agreement, and asked President Reagan to explore this with Congress. By October 1987 the elements of an agreement had been reached, and both governments subsequently gave approval. The issue played a key role in the Canadian election in the fall of 1988, which the Conservatives won. The agreement came into effect at the beginning of 1989.

Two reasons stand out in the government's desire to pursue such a course. One was defensive: the desire to avoid both short- and long-term losses. The Canadian government decided to take out more insurance, having found most of Canada's eggs in one basket—a basket which was proving to be quite unsteady at times. A smaller country's tactic, in such circumstances, is often to try to commit the larger one to agreed and enforceable rules of trade and other ties.

The United States by 1986 accounted for three-quarters of Canada's exports, as against two-thirds in 1971 and half in 1961. Thanks particularly to the Autopact, fully 90 percent of manufactured exports went to the United States. Over 70 percent of Canada's fast-rising outward direct investment was in the United States in the mid-1980s. Canadians were concerned about growing U.S. protectionism in trade and investment. Sometimes that was directed at Canada, but even when it was not, it could still do serious damage to that country. For example, the jobs lost in Canada as a result of a hypothetical trade war between the United States and other major countries has been estimated by one study at a figure close to the entire loss in jobs in Canadian manufacturing during the recent recession.[1] Of course, new forms of trade protection grew elsewhere in the 1980s, but these were not Canada's main markets.[2] And Canada was sensitive to the fact that its own protectionist experiments in investment and energy in the late 1970s and early 1980s triggered a very strong U.S. reaction before these policies were scaled down.

The other important reason for pursuing a trade pact was more forward-looking. A number of studies pointed to the likelihood of significant economic gains in overall output, notably through rationalization of production in a manufacturing industry which, in many sectors, was still well below attainable levels of productivity. Those studies recognized that there were losses in low-skill, labor-intensive sectors in particular from a trade pact, but elsewhere the adjustment should lead fairly quickly to restructured plants and new technologies and skills that would enhance competitiveness at the international level. Thus the unavoidable adjustments to global restructuring would, it was believed, be facilitated within a phased bilateral arrangement with Canada's major trade and investment partner. More broadly, it was recognized that the traditional reliance on natural resources had to be complemented, given long-term declining terms of trade, with a more efficient manufacturing sector and surer market access for both goods and the rapidly growing services sector.[3]

One can point to a variety of other political and economic reasons for the Canadian government's decision on the FTA. Some would see it as the desire of a Conservative government, wedded to the ideas of deregulation and privatization, to pursue equivalent free-market approaches in the area of trade policy. It is not clear how important this motive was, in view of the relatively modest deregulation and privatization which did occur; the fact that the Liberal government, which lost power in 1984, had already sharply changed course on its more interventionist policies; and the existence of many safeguards and exceptions in both the FTA and NAFTA. Personalities and the political opportunities available to leaders at any given time may have been as important as the issues of principle.

EFFECTS OF THE FTA: REMAINING PROBLEMS

What has been the outcome, from Canada's perspective? Conclusions must be tentative, since it is difficult to be precise about a policy whose effects can be assessed only in the longerterm. In economic terms the results are probably about as expected, and positive on balance. In broader terms, the FTA has been costly and has left a number of issues in its wake that are important to NAFTA as well.

On the economic aspects, the restructuring of manufacturing in particular has proceeded rapidly—pushed, no doubt, by the early 1990s recession. There is considerable evidence of both export and import growth (despite recessions in both countries), as one would expect of the FTA pressure for specialization, so that Canadian firms lost market share in the domestic market but gained market share in the United States. These trends are far more evident in the Canada-U.S. context than in Canada's overseas trade. Manufacturing productivity increased greatly, despite the recession. Direct business investment increased both into and out of Canada, but especially from overseas. There has been much sectoral exit and entry as firms reduce costs by changing product lines, leaving some businesses and markets and developing others.[4]

Politically, the FTA was a disaster for the Conservative party, despite that party's electoral win in 1988, and despite the fact that neither the FTA nor the NAFTA played a major role in the election of October 1993—though the New Democratic party and some other organizations tried hard to focus public attention on the issue. The FTA will probably keep coming back in one form or another for several reasons.

There are at least two major problems with how the FTA was developed, one related to the nature of the deal and the other to the Canadian government's attitude toward implementing it.[5] A major objective of the Canadian government, to improve access to U.S. markets by better handling of the surge of anti-dumping and subsidy-countervail cases, was only partly resolved. The FTA did replace domestic appeal systems with binational review panels. Each party applies its own laws, but the panels decide whether these are applied correctly and fairly. This is a considerable improvement over what existed before, at least from a Canadian perspective. However, it falls far short of the Canadian government's objective, which was to assure access by finding an alternative to anti-dumping (probably through competition policy) and some harmonization of subsidy law. The proportion of Canada-U.S. trade subject to such protective devices is not large. Nevertheless, the way in which private groups in the United States can repeatedly target imports of a product through trade remedies has led to much skepticism about the treaty, since the uncertainty of access would appear to erode one of the main motives Canada had for entering negotiations. This is, one may note, a global issue. From 1980 to 1990 almost 1,400 anti-dumping actions were initiated under the GATT, and they appear to have increased in the subsequent recession. European countries have recently used this weapon very extensively, and it is not uncommon in Canada. In the same period 481 countervailing cases were launched, 278 in the United States alone.[6]

The second issue is much broader. Any major policy agreement such as the FTA, even between two industrialized countries, imposes downward adjustment pressures on some industries, regions, and factors of production, and provides upward adjustment opportunities for others. Many of the changes are internal to multinational firms (although cross-border) and intra-industry, and hence may occur more rapidly than otherwise, but the problems in some sectors are significant nonetheless. The government of Canada, supported by the report of a special committee, took the view that it would not offer special adjustment programs in addition to those already in existence. Its argument was that it was difficult to distinguish those harmed by the FTA from those harmed by other developments, and, in any case, some of Canada's major public adjustment support programs are more generous than those in the United States (though not those of some European countries). The government also appeared unwilling to admit that the FTA would harm some groups significantly. Many people disagreed, including many economists who had produced research favoring freer trade.[7] Where public policies improve overall welfare but harm some groups, there is a case for using some of the gains to assist those who lose to adjust more quickly or less painfully. Governments have insisted in recent years that private businesses be aware of and responsive to the social costs of business policies. Is government to be exempted from this responsibility?

In strictly political terms it was a mistake to take this attitude. Many people sensed the inherent unfairness of the government's position. The mistake was compounded by exaggerated claims, not least from Prime Minister Brian Mulroney but supported by some researchers, of large gains, notably in jobs. In the context of a serious recession with substantial job losses reflecting a variety of causes, such claims were easily attacked. We know, or should know, that trade policy is directed to wealth gains over time, which implies better-paid jobs rather than overall job gains. We also know, or should know, that trade policy is not the same thing as growth policy, which requires private or public saving and investment (especially investments in human capital and innovations) over time. Liberalized market access and the pressures of import competition serve as a spur to increased business competitiveness and growth, but whether that growth is achieved on a continuing basis depends on these broader decisions.

All of this mattered little once the political process took hold of the issues. Many Canadians are firmly convinced that most of the substantial number of job losses in the past several years are directly due to the FTA. No matter that the serious studies on the subject, tentative as they must be at this stage, suggest that 15 percent of the job losses in manufacturing at the maximum are likely to be due to the FTA, with the rest reflecting tax increases, the recession in the United States, overshooting of the inflation-reduction targets of monetary policy, relative wage-rate changes, longer-term structural adjustments, and other factors.[8] Perhaps the most important continuing effect in the political arena was the public's distrust of the Conservative government on this point (among others) and the propensity of the Liberal party to suggest it would reopen parts of the FTA, and reconsider the NAFTA once it returned to power. These treaties were not a major issue in the 1993 elections, except for the New Democrats and some marginal political parties. Along with the recession and the attempts to revise the constitution, however, they did contribute to the remarkable embitterment of the Canadian political scene in recent years. This was especially so in Ontario, where both the Liberal and New Democratic provincial governments have been opposed to the FTA, and the latter has declared it will challenge the NAFTA in the courts as an intrusion into areas of provincial jurisdiction.

ENTER THE NAFTA

Canada's reasons for entering the discussions on the NAFTA were more complex than those with regard to the FTA. The economic gains are not as clear, given the small volume of trade and investment involved. Direct trade with Mexico, for example, is only about 1 percent of Canada's overall trade, and most tariffs on imports are already low. Most estimates suggest very small Canadian gains overall, although they are subject to more than the usual uncertainty given the present scale of contact between Canada and Mexico, the problems of measuring dynamic changes over time, the fact that high- and low-income countries are involved, and the likelihood of losses in some traditional manufacturing sectors.[9]

Why would the Canadian government enter negotiations in these circumstances? Again, the reasons were partly defensive and partly forward-looking. Canada was anxious to preserve and, if possible, extend both the U.S. access already secured and the protection built in for cultural and other sectors. Sitting on the sidelines might not have assured this. The one likely result of not participating was a "hub-and-spoke" outcome. In other words, if the United States made separate bilateral deals with Canada, Mexico, and others, it would be the only country whose firms had access to each market—a fact that firms deciding on investment locations would take into account along with the other determinants of investment decisions.[10]

The other reason for Canadian participation stems from the realization that multinational firms are going to restructure production in any case. The relevant question is whether and how fast a trading country such as Canada moves toward the kind of economy which emphasizes investment in human capital and innovation so that firms can compete internationally. Protection for industries with unskilled labor gives the wrong signals to capital and labor—it reduces the returns to higher-skilled workers and to capital (hence reducing incentives to acquiring skills), and it increases employment in lower-paid jobs. This is a dangerous situation for a small, open economy under any circumstances. It is more so in a context where multinational firms, wherever owned, are restructuring their production and distribution systems on a regional or even a global basis. While some Canadians would like to slow or even stop this process, the chances of doing so are slight: even if we could persuade Canadian-based multinationals to rely on exports and not direct investment, for example, they would begin to lose out to other multinationals which took advantage of Mexico and other sites as markets and as sources for certain types of components and supplies.

Ultimately, the case for the NAFTA is that it gives Canadian firms a more secure and dynamic context in which to make the inevitable adjustments to industry rationalization, whether for older or newer sectors. Studies of the location decisions of multinational firms in response to the increased import and export opportunities which go with trade liberalization suggest two conclusions. One is that there is no wholesale closure of plants and exit from one country to another; indeed, both inward and outward direct investment may increase for a time. The other conclusion, however, is that a good deal of changeover occurs at the plant level and, in some sectors, in terms of the size of the industry. Firms will specialize their product lines, change supplier relations, reorganize nonproduction functions, and so on, with consequences both for the nature of their workforce and perhaps for their ownership structure. It is difficult to say much about all of this without looking at particular multinationals and industries. Let us concentrate on the issue of Canada's attraction as a site for direct investment, whether by Canadian or foreign multinationals, and the choices available in the FTA and the NAFTA. One can then make a case that Canada's interests would be best served, in descending order, by (1) FTA only, (2) NAFTA only, (3) FTA plus a Mexico-U.S. "hub-and-spoke" model, (4) no bilateral agreements, and (5) a Mexico-U.S. agreement without an FTA. If the United States and Mexico alone had made a deal, that would have ruled out (1) and (4), leaving (2) as the preferred outcome.[11] Some Canadians still insist that (3) and even (5) are superior to (2) despite the probable investment losses involved.

The process of approving the NAFTA proved to be fraught with difficulty in both the United States and Canada, but particularly the former. Canadians might have watched the debate in the United States with wry amusement—just a rerun of the open-ended debate in Canada on the FTA, but with the United States experiencing the alarms, both real and imagined—except that Canadian interests came under pressure in various ways. The environmental and labor side deals opened up some interesting challenges for Canada, quite apart from the potentially far-reaching effects on all three countries from investing powers (albeit constrained) in new trilateral organizations. Canada's strong concerns that appeals to these organizations would deteriorate into yet another avenue for protection led to its being exempted from the threat of trade sanctions. Persistent failure to enforce environmental and labor laws can lead to a "monetary enforcement assessment." Failure to pay this or to enforce its laws can lead, in the case of Mexico and the United States, to suspension of NAFTA benefits based on the amount of the assessment. In the case of Canada, however, proceedings are begun before a Canadian court to collect the assessment and to secure an action plan.

Perhaps more far-reaching are the exemptions to the side deals in recognition of provincial areas of jurisdiction. The provinces have substantial powers in environmental issues and are responsible for most labor legislation. In areas of provincial jurisdiction, the side agreements take effect only if provinces representing at least 55 percent and 35 percent of gross domestic product ratify the side deal, in the case of environmental and labor issues, respectively. At the same time, if the provinces do not accept the procedures involved in the side deals, the Canadian government will be constrained in taking action against Mexico or the United States in the case of practices which would be under provincial jurisdiction if performed in Canada.

These special provisions for Canada may simply reflect the fact that the side deals were actually aimed by the United States at Mexico's uneven enforcement of its labor and environmental standards. They do raise a larger issue, however. The FTA and the NAFTA are already very comprehensive in the topics covered. One of the provisions which makes these treaties acceptable to many Canadians is the recourse to national treatment, which preserves each country's laws and regulations so long as they do not discriminate against firms owned in the other countries. Another type of provision is to explicitly exclude certain issues, such as health services. The attempt to move from barriers at the border to "deeper integration" is understandable but highly problematic. A great variety of domestic polices affect international trade, and hence lead those in other countries who are affected negatively to press for policy harmonization. This pressure raises many difficult issues: whose standards will be used for harmonization, how different countries can express their policy preferences in the face of such pressures, what supranational institutions must be put in place to enforce such harmonization, and so on. Small countries are not likely to be enthusiastic about such deeper integration when their main trading partner is as powerful as the United States. The European Union is sometimes cited as an example of such integration, but it embodies a set of political objectives, common standards, and common institutions which few in Canada would favor. Perhaps the point can be driven home for an American audience by asking how they would react to a Canadian complaint of unfair trade practices by many U.S. states whose labor legislation is far less developed than that in Canada. As Sylvia Ostry has noted, the real questions are whether limited economic integration will create pressures for deeper integration, and whether the United States will use trade policy unilaterally for such purposes?[12]

The dramatic battle to win congressional approval for the NAFTA raised yet another range of issues for Canada. In the race to line up votes in favor of the NAFTA, there were concerns that the implementing legislation would undo parts of the FTA (such as cultural protection and dispute settlement procedures) or lead to new protective measures (for example, against imports of durum wheat).[13] For a time, it appeared the NAFTA might fail to be approved, and it is of interest to speculate briefly on the consequences. I would guess that the newly elected Liberal government would have heaved a collective (but not unanimous) sigh of relief and gratefully let the issue fade away. I have already indicated why I believe the Conservative government was lukewarm about the NAFTA; one could hardly expect more from the Liberals, who had strong reservations about the FTA, which (for Canada) was at the heart of the NAFTA. There was brief speculation that, in the event of failure to secure U.S. approval of the NAFTA, Canada might propose a bilateral deal with Mexico.[14] It seems highly unlikely that any Canadian government would have been prepared to take such a bold step.

The consequences for the United States and the world of such a failure would have been difficult to predict, but might have been far-reaching. The damage to the presidency of Bill Clinton might have been long-lasting. It would likely have strengthened the hand of those in the United States who favor protectionist approaches to trade policy, and perhaps would have delayed the adjustments U.S. industry is undergoing as it struggles to maintain its competitive strength. It might well have weakened attempts to complete the GATT, if only because of the reluctance of other parties to make concessions to an Administration which appeared to have problems in securing congressional approval.

It has been said that foreign policy is an instrument of trade policy in a small, open economy such as Canada's, where foreign trade plays such a major role in economic activity. In the United States, with its many and diverse international responsibilities, it may be more correct to say that trade policy is an instrument of foreign policy. If the U.S. government had not been able to close a deal with its small and economically less developed neighbor, how would it be expected to close a deal with Japan, the EU (especially France!), and the many other large and small countries in the GATT? The consequences of a failure to approve the NAFTA would, of course, have been felt most strongly in Mexico and in Latin America. Perhaps the economic effects, narrowly defined, might not have been the more lasting ones. Export prices can be adjusted downward to surmount tariffs, and other modifications are possible if a trade agreement fails. The negative message to the movement for reform in Latin America might have been the more lasting and highly damaging consequence.

But the NAFTA did secure congressional approval, thereby posing some problems in Canada, where the Conservative party had been reduced to two members in the House of Commons and the Liberal party formed the government.

ENTER CANADA

The Liberal government elected in October 1993 had taken a cautiously critical view of the NAFTA. As noted earlier, this issue and the FTA did not figure prominently in the Liberal party's policy stance during the election, although the emphasis on job creation certainly did form an important aspect of the attack on the economic policies of the Conservative government. What the Liberals did emphasize was the need to reopen various parts of the NAFTA agreement before considering its proclamation.[15]

The Liberal party's concerns can be summarized under the headings of trade rules, natural resources, labor, and the environment. The Canadian government was concerned that appeals to the new trilateral organizations on labor and the environment would generate new avenues for protection. As noted above, these concerns were partly met by the exemptions given to Canada. With regard to the rules for settlement of trade disputes, what came into effect with the FTA was better than what existed before. Nevertheless, the two countries had failed to agree on ways to harmonize rules on anti-dumping and the application of subsidy-countervail. This was left to negotiations over a five-year period ending in December 1993, with the possibility of a two-year renewal. Working groups were set up in 1989 on these issues, but during the NAFTA negotiations it was agreed to set these discussions aside. The continued use of existing rules to impede trade has been a target for much criticism of the FTA in Canada. In any event, the three countries have now agreed to nonbinding efforts in two working groups over two years, so as to define codes or agreements on the use of subsidy-countervail and anti-dumping measures. These efforts are likely to be superseded, in the case of subsidy-countervail, by what was achieved in the Uruguay Round of GATT, if this becomes law. However, little progress was made in the GATT in improving the use of anti-dumping measures.

On the resources issue, the Canadian government clarified its position on energy by declaring that it would interpret and apply the NAFTA in a way which maximizes energy security for Canadians, and would also take any necessary measures, including the establishment of strategic reserves. Whether this has any effect remains to be seen: it is a unilateral declaration whose application could be contested by the other parties. The three countries also stated that the NAFTA does not require that a country either exploit its water for commercial use and hence be subject to the usual rules governing trade) or that it begin exporting water in any form. There is some question of whether there was any doubt about this.[16]

TRADE DIVERSION IN THE NAFTA

It was suggested earlier that there were substantive reasons for a Canadian government to go along with the NAFTA, despite the apparently small overall economic effects. Failure to ratify would not have prevented the competitive improvements involved for firms in the United States and especially in Mexico, while Canada would have given up the improvements made possible by the treaty. A number of specific improvements can be cited, such as the mechanisms to avoid or resolve disputes (automobiles, financial services, and investment generally) and better access to government procurement—quite apart from enlarged access to the Mexican market on a broad front.[17]

That being said, it is also clear that some provisions of the NAFTA can be considered restrictive and discriminatory. This issue can be considered broadly or narrowly. From a broad perspective, while all such arrangements between a few countries necessarily involve some trade diversion as well as trade creation, the NAFTA is unlikely to qualify as one of those with significant diversion. From a narrower perspective, some of the sectoral arrangements are difficult to justify in a treaty developed to liberalize trade.

On the general impact, it is worth noting that removing restrictions between several countries and adopting common rules of origin necessarily divert some trade to higher-cost members of the group at the expense of other countries. One can make a strong case that the FTA in particular, and the NAFTA which took over many of its provisions, were less likely to create such diversion because of their structure. The FTA was modeled in large part on the GATT, including provisions being discussed in the Uruguay Round. Both the FTA and the NAFTA are very comprehensive, including trade in goods and services, rules on investment, intellectual property, and many other issues, some going well beyond what was concluded in the Uruguay Round. And, on tariffs and related measures, what is involved is a free-trade area with separate national tariffs against other countries. There was no attempt to bargain up tariffs against other countries, as can happen in negotiations on a customs union with a common tariff. Indeed, the pressure from the private sector tends to lead to the lowering of external tariffs, since differential tariffs raise production costs and damage competitiveness. Those member countries which believe they suffer from trade diversion have the option of lowering their tariffs against nonmembers. Finally, the external tariff is relatively low, particularly in the case of the United States.

It should be added that any move toward a customs union in the NAFTA is likely to be resisted by the two smaller countries, Canada and Mexico. It is true that trade diversion will lessen when the three NAFTA countries cut their tariffs in the Uruguay Round. It has also been suggested that adverse trade effects might be smaller if the three countries adopted a common external tariff, thus removing concerns about transshipment of foreign components among them.[18] The problem here is that the setting of a common external tariff and related rules is likely to be dominated by the United States. Canadians (and perhaps Mexicans), who are already heavily dependent on the United States, may wonder why they should increase that dependency. Small and large countries have different ways of looking at trade policy, as already noted. And both Canada and Mexico have had reasons for differing significantly from U.S. trade policies in the past, notwithstanding its relatively low external tariff. This is one aspect of the issue of deepening integration discussed earlier.

Finally, in terms of the general impact, one should note that a regional trade agreement can lead to trade creation as well as diversion. This can occur to the extent that the agreement raises income levels in one or more member countries, and thereby raises overall imports into the region. More particularly, it is the trade diversion to Mexico which is feared by some countries, given that its tariffs are the highest of the three member countries. Yet it is also Mexico which is likely to experience the largest relative increase in its real income, and perhaps in its growth rate as well. In that case the effects on imports of the expansion of the Mexican market may well swamp the trade diversion effects.

Turning to specific sectors, one can point to benefits to non-NAFTA residents, such as the extension to them of the liberalization of services trade and of investment regulation. However, in some important sectors the rules of origin have been set in ways which could involve significant trade diversion.[19] The standard rule of origin is that goods from non-NAFTA countries will qualify for preferential treatment if they undergo "substantial transformation" in the region, and hence move to another tariff classification. In automobiles and parts, the FTA requirement of 50 percent value added has been raised to between 60 and 62.5 percent, and tracing requirements are set in place to assure that the new content requirements are met. The effect is a considerable increase in North American content requirements in order to qualify for preferential treatment. In textiles and apparel a triple transformation test is introduced, with some exceptions. The effect is to increase the protectionist rules of the FTA in this sector in ways which are complex and sometimes bizarre.

Any overall evaluation of the NAFTA must await the test of time, as well as fuller models of the effects on both members and non-members. The treaty involves a considerable range of liberalization, as well as some protectionist backsliding and elements of unfinished business. President Clinton gave the right message in his speeches urging approval on the basis of the benefits involved. He also went on to emphasize that better training, retraining, and reemployment programs must accompany the NAFTA and the many other economic changes which are increasing the insecurity of some sectors and groups; and that trade policy alone will not secure continuing improvement in living standards and a better job performance. Such issues were not dealt with well in the Canadian debate. We shall see which country lives up to these challenges more fully and wisely in the future.

CONCLUSION

In economic terms, the Canadian government's reasons for proposing the FTA were partly defensive—to avoid the losses likely from any trade war involving its major trading partner—and partly related to the likelihood of significant efficiency gains from increased rationalization of production. The probable economic results for Canada are likely to be positive over time, although short of some of the forecasts. In political terms the treaty was a disaster for the Conservative government, despite its electoral victory in 1988.

In part the difficulties reflected the coincidence of the onset of a recession (in the United States as well as in Canada) shortly after the treaty went into effect. For many Canadians the heavy loss of manufacturing jobs in the early 1990s was largely, if incorrectly, associated with the FTA. There were also defects in both the substance and the implementation of the FTA from Canada's perspective. A small country is clearly going to have to make significant concessions in order to secure guaranteed access to the market of a very large trading partner. The problem was that the treaty failed to assure such access to the U.S. market in some important respects, notably the use of subsidy-countervail and anti-dumping measures. The government also failed to acknowledge and give adequate attention to the groups which suffered losses from the unavoidable adjustments required by trade liberalization.

There were important lessons here for the subsequent debate in the United States on the desirability of implementing the NAFTA or, indeed, any other policy which has far-reaching and uneven effects on groups of people. Every effort should be made to design policies which are optimal—in itself a formidable task, given the pressure of competing interests and values. But even the best-designed policies can be derailed if governments raise expectations which prove to be, or even appear to be, false. The Canadian government's insistence that large job gains would result from the FTA was clearly false in principle, and quickly ran into the problem of explaining subsequent job losses. In addition, the failure to acknowledge clearly and to deal with the costs of complex policy changes led to political embitterment on a wider front.

Canada's reasons for entering the discussions on the NAFTA were also defensive in part, particularly a desire to preserve the gains and the exemptions of the FTA. In part, too, the NAFTA gives Canadian firms a more secure and dynamic context in which to adjust to the ongoing pressures for industry rationalizations, pressures from both North America and overseas markets and from a variety of technical changes. The NAFTA did not lead to the same intense debate in Canada as did the FTA, largely because Canada's direct trade and investment links with Mexico are still small. The side agreements on labor and environmental issues were aimed more at Mexico's enforcement of its laws. The newly elected Liberal government had hoped to reopen some of the terms of the FTA and was critical of the NAFTA side agreements. It had to settle for some minor concessions before proclaiming the NAFTA.

The successful conclusion of the FTA and NAFTA, along with the Uruguay Round, leaves some important issues for any subsequent regional or global trade discussions. The FTA and NAFTA involve a deeper degree of integration than was achieved in many aspects of the Uruguay Round. Examples are investment regulation, and the labor and environmental side agreements. Closer economic associations, such as the EU, have gone much further. The arguments regarding the desirability of deeper integration are likely to dominate future trade policy discussions.

NOTES

1. Economic Council of Canada, *Supply and Services* (Ottawa: the Council, 1986), pp. 24, 85. See also G. W. Harrison and E. E. Rutström, "Trade Wars, Trade Negotiations and Applied Game Theory," *Economic Journal*, May 1991, 420-35.

2. The growth of nontariff barriers is outlined in A. E. Safarian, "Direct Investment Issues for the 1990s: An Overview," in Mari Pangestu, ed., *Pacific*

Initiatives for Regional Trade Liberalization and Investment Co-operation (Jakarta: Centre for Strategic and International Studies, 1993), pp. 107-11. Briefly, factor protection through fiscal incentives such as subsidies has shown a rising trend over time. In addition, the use of several types of commodity protection has increased sharply, notably anti-dumping and subsidy-countervail. In the period 1980-86, four countries or regions accounted for almost all of the anti-dumping cases under GATT: the United States (30 percent), Australia (27 percent), Canada (22 percent), and the EC (19 percent). Fully 58 percent of countervail cases were initiated in this period by the United States (92 percent if Chile is left out of the data).

3. There is a good short statement of these developments in Richard G. Harris, *Trade, Money and Wealth in the Canadian Economy* (Toronto: C. D. Howe Institute, 1993). Two of the more important studies of the impact of freer trade are P. Wonnacott and R. J. Wonnacott, *Free Trade Between Canada and The United States* (Cambridge, Mass.: Harvard University Press, 1967); and Richard G. Harris, Trade, Industrial Policy and Canadian Manufacturing (Toronto: Economic Council of Canada, 1983). For a longer statement of motives, see A. E. Safarian, "Introductory Comments," in G. Bertin and A. Raynauld, *Economic Integration in Europe and North America* (Paris: Clément Juglar, 1992).

4. For data on these trends, see, for example, Daniel Schwanen, *A Growing Success: Canada's Performance Under Free Trade*, Commentary no. 52 (Toronto: C. D. Howe Institute Commentary, No. 52, September 1993; Statistics Canada, *Trade Patterns: Canada-United States* (Ottawa: Statistics Canada, 1993); and J. Baldwin and M. Rafiquzzaman, "Structural Change in the Canadian Manufacturing Sector," working paper (Ottawa: Statistics Canada, 1993), mimeo.

5. Some believed it was a mistake to include so many items in the deal, and preferred a strictly goods-and-tariff approach of the Kennedy Round. Given the breadth of the Uruguay Round, and the interrelation of goods, investment, and services issues, it is difficult to see how a narrow agreement would have been of significant benefit to Canada. Nor would it likely have been acceptable to the United States, which saw a broad deal as a way of putting pressure on others to implement the Uruguay Round.

6. Sylvia Ostry, "Free Trade and the Canadian Experience," presentation to the Americas Society, Montreal, June 16-19, 1993, p. 3. She goes on to note that these special dispute settlement procedures of the FTA and the NAFTA do not apply to section 301 of the 1988 U.S. Omnibus Trade Act.

7. See, for example, R. J. Wonnacott, *Canadian and U.S. Adjustment Policies in a Bilateral Trade Agreement* (Toronto: C. D. Howe Institute, 1987).

8. For a discussion of five studies of job losses, see Leonard Waverman,

"The NAFTA Agreement: a Canadian Perspective," in S. Globerman and Walker (eds.). Assessing NAFTA: A Transnational Analysis (Vancouver: Fraser Institute, 1993), p. 39-50. See also Peter Dungan, Steve Murphy, and Thomas Wilson, "Sources of the Recession in Canada and Ontario," Policy Study 93-5 (Toronto: Institute for Policy Analysis, University of Toronto, 1993).

9. See, for example, the three studies outlined in U.S. International Trade Commission, *Economy-Wide Modelling of the Economic Implications of an FTA with Mexico and a NAFTA with Canada and Mexico* (Washington, D.C.: The Commission, 1992). A study by Jim Standford of the Brookings Institution, reported in the *Toronto Globe and Mail*, October 1, 1993, p. B3, suggests, by contrast, that Canada's GDP will fall by 1.5 percent, while GDP will soar in Mexico and not be much affected in the United States. The potential for dynamic changes over time is brought out in the studies noted in William O. Watson, *The Economic Impact of the NAFTA* (Toronto: C. D. Howe Institute, 1993).

10. See R. G. Lipsey, *Canada at the U.S.-Mexico Free Trade Dance: Wallflower or Partner?* and R. J. Wonnacott, *Canada and the U.S.-Mexico Free Trade Negotiations* (Toronto: C. D. Howe Institute, 1990).

11. These comments are not an evaluation of the specific terms of the NAFTA with regard to investment, which have been criticized by many writers as far too riddled with exemptions. The reaction of multinationals to trade liberalization is further discussed in Harris, *Trade, Money and Wealth*, pp. 24-29; B. Curtis Eaton, Richard G. Lipsey, and A. Edward Safarian, "The Theory of Multinational Plant Location in a Regional Trading Area," and Lorraine Eden, "Who Does What After NAFTA? Location Strategies of Multinationals," both in Lorraine Eden, ed., *Multinationals in North America* (Calgary: University of Calgary Press, 1994).

12. Ostry, "Free Trade and Canada," pp. 5-7.

13. See *Toronto Globe and Mail*, October 19, 1993, article by James Bovard, reprinted from the *Wall Street Journal*, and November 4, 1993, article by Drew Fagan and John Saunders.

14. See Giles Gherson, *Toronto Globe and Mail*, November 13, 1993.

15. The agreement had already been approved by Parliament, but the final legal step of proclamation was necessary.

16. The opposing views on this are conveyed in articles by Jamie Linton and Lawrence L. Herman, *Toronto Globe and Mail*, November 19, 1993.

17. See, for example, Richard G. Lipsey, Daniel Schwanen and Ronald J. Wonnacott, *Inside or Outside the NAFTA?* (Toronto: C. D. Howe Institute, 1993).

18. See G. L. Hufbauer and J. J. Schott, eds., *NAFTA: An Assessment* (Washington, D.C.: Institute for International Economics, 1993), p. 6. The

issues in this and preceding paragraphs are dealt with more fully in Eaton, Lipsey and Safarian, "The Theory of Multinational Plant Location."

19. See Hufbauer and Schott, *NAFTA*, pp. 5-7, 37-46. It has been argued that the sectoral arrangements noted here, along with measures favoring other sectors in competition with non-NAFTA producers, can be interpreted as the beginnings of a discriminatory North American industrial policy. See Michael Gestrin and Alan Rugman, "The Impact of NAFTA upon North American Investment Patterns," forthcoming in *Transnational Corporations*.

3

NAFTA and Foreign Direct Investment in the United States

Alvin Paul Drischler

Although largely ignored in the debate surrounding the NAFTA agreement, foreign direct investment in the United States (FDIUS) is of increasing significance to key sectors and important regions of the American economy. While conclusive empirical data are likely to remain unavailable for some time and a whole host of variables are involved, the move in the direction of a single market occasioned by the NAFTA provides some preliminary indications of largely positive effects on direct investment by nonparties in the United States.

FDIUS

The United States has dominated global foreign investment since the end of World War II, originating over 40 percent of foreign direct investment (FDI) as late as the second half of the 1970s.[1] By the end of the 1980s, the United States had also become the largest single recipient of FDI. Today, it is both the largest recipient and the most significant source of FDI.[2]

The growth in FDIUS has correlated closely with a number of global trends. Among the most pronounced of these is an increasing emphasis on manufacturing and services, as opposed to the extraction of natural resources. Within manufacturing, much of the increase in FDIUS can be attributed to the globalization of the world economy as foreign firms increasingly have moved production facilities offshore to ensure overseas market penetration, take advantage of cost differentials, or achieve economies of scale on a global basis. Much of the growth of FDIUS in the services sector has been driven by deregulation in the financial, insurance and telecommunications industries, where the United States has taken a particularly strong leadership role.

Other factors encouraging growth in FDIUS have been high rates of economic growth in the United States relative to other industrialized countries in the 1980s, and a depreciation of the dollar against key currencies such as the yen and the D-mark. The relatively open U.S. investment climate, combined with the threat of import restrictions, especially on Japanese automakers, also encouraged more foreign direct investment in the United States in the 1980s.

Although still a relatively small part of the massive U.S. economy, FDIUS is growing in importance both by region and industry sector. As Tables 3.1 and 3.2 indicate, FDIUS annual inflows increased from $11.5 billion in 1983 to $69 billion in 1989. Despite a more recent reduction in this rate of growth, year-end values of FDI stock increased from $126 billion to $487 billion during the period from 1981 to 1991, an increase of 286 percent in a decade.

Table 3.1
FDIUS (1980-91) Flows (book value, billions of dollars)

1980	16.9	1986	36.1
1981	25.2	1987	59.6
1982	13.8	1988	58.6
1983	11.5	1989	69.0
1984	25.6	1990	46.1
1985	20.5	1991	12.6

Source: U.S. Department of Commerce, June 1993.

Table 3.2
FDIUS (1980-91) Stock (tangible assets at replacement value, billions of dollars)

1980	126
1985	231
1991	487

Source: Department of Commerce, June 1993.

Despite some ebbing in the rate of growth in FDIUS in the early 1990s, inward foreign investment is beginning to have a significant overall impact in the United States and an even greater impact in specific sectors and regions. By 1990 foreign affiliates accounted for 12 percent of domestic manufacturing sales and 37 percent of sales in the wholesale trade sector.[3] In addition, affiliates were responsible for 7 percent of total banking employment and over 11 percent of total manufacturing employment.[4]

Affiliates play an even more significant role in the manufacturing output of several states. In 1991, affiliates accounted for 37 percent of the total manufacturing output in Delaware, 36 percent in West Virginia, 24 percent in New Jersey, and 19 percent each in Georgia, South Carolina, and North Carolina.

Data on affiliate employment further reveal the importance of FDIUS by state and region. In 1991, nonbank affiliates provided 555,000 jobs in California, 362,000 jobs in New York, and 310,000 jobs in Texas.[5] The importance of FDIUS to manufacturing employment is even greater for several other states, on a percentage basis: 21.6 percent of all manufacturing jobs in West Virginia, 20.6 percent in Delaware, 17.6 percent in Alaska, 17 percent in South Carolina, and over 15 percent each in Kentucky, New Jersey, and Maryland.[6] For each state, the high percentage of affiliate-related manufacturing employment is due to domination by foreign-owned firms in that state's major industries, such as the chemical and mining industries in West Virginia, the chemical industry in Delaware, and the fish and seafood processing industry in Alaska.[7]

FDIUS is now so important that attracting it has become the cornerstone of economic development plans in every region of the United States and the object of intense competition among subnational governments at all levels. To attract foreign direct investment and the additional jobs and tax revenues that go with it, states, cities, and counties throughout the United States have resorted to extensive incentive packages. These packages most often rely on substantial tax breaks or holidays and other financial inducements, such as below-market-rate financing vehicles. On a broader scale, incentive packages have included as well the establishment of worker training and employment assistance programs, infrastructure improvements, land grants or leases, and extensive site selection and market information assistance.

Whether the use of incentives succeeds in attracting direct investment, and whether the returns justify the costs, are highly controversial questions. However, in the course of their competition to attract foreign direct investment, subnational governments in the United States have learned that FDI decisions involve a host of political and economic variables considerably more complicated than a simple comparison of labor costs.

Although not referring to external investors directly, President Clinton underscored some of the most important considerations likely to affect North American investment decisions by external investors when he said during the NAFTA debate, "businesses do not choose to locate based solely on wages . . . businesses do choose to locate based on the skills and the productivity of the work force, the attitude of the government, the roads and the railroads to deliver products, the availability of a market close enough to make the transportation costs meaningful, and the communications networks necessary to support the enterprise."[8]

A complete assessment of the process by which multinational firms make direct investment decisions is considerably beyond the scope of this chapter. Suffice it to say that firms headquartered outside North America are likely to consider a wide variety of economic, political, cultural, and demographic factors in deciding whether and where to invest in North America. The precise impact of the NAFTA agreement on all these factors will never be easy to measure. Nevertheless, if NAFTA is considered as a step toward a single market in North America, we can begin to derive some preliminary indications as to its likely effect on external investors and FDIUS.

The NAFTA debate in the U.S. Congress in the fall of 1993 dealt only indirectly with the likely impact of the agreement on FDIUS. The focus instead was on U.S. investment and the likelihood of a loss of U.S. jobs to Mexico, which opponents contended would follow from lower wage rates and lax environmental and worker safety standards south of the border.

Of course, whether U.S. investors might be lured to Mexico as a result of the NAFTA and whether NAFTA might similarly divert external investors to locate in Mexico rather than the United States are not unrelated. As U.S. investors might be attracted to Mexico by lower labor costs or more relaxed environmental standards, so these same factors might similarly divert European and Japanese investors from the United States to Mexico, with adverse consequences for FDIUS and the U.S. economy.

During the debate, proponents contended that long-term comparative advantage would affect investment allocations far more than the terms of the NAFTA. They argued that the U.S. economy was shifting away from low-skill, low-paid jobs to higher-value-added and more advanced production methods. Some U.S. firms might choose to invest in Mexico, but these would be largely in low wage, manufacturing sectors where the jobs would likely be lost by the United States regardless of NAFTA, as part of the increasing globalization of the world economy and greater international competition.

It is far too early to judge with certainty how external investors will integrate the many complex factors involved in considering direct investment decisions in North America. Even so, some preliminary insights can be gleaned if NAFTA is understood as a step toward a single market in North America. Though not as advanced and having much different structural characteristics than the European Union (EU), NAFTA can be seen as a movement toward a single large market in North America with freer flow of goods, persons, services, and capital.

NAFTA extends and expands to Mexico basic investment provisions on national treatment and limitations on performance requirements contained in the Canada-U.S. Free Trade Agreement. Other provisions include stronger intellectual property protection, a more open services market, and better access to the government procurement process.

NAFTA commits all three countries to give national treatment or better to investors from NAFTA parties. The NAFTA provisions on investment apply to all investors in the North American region, including companies controlled by non-North American owners.[9] Like Mexican, Canadian, or American companies, foreign enterprises with established operations in North America can also enjoy preferential treatment, thereby affording foreign investors increased security for their investments in the region. Non-NAFTA enterprises can receive the benefits of the NAFTA investment provisions only if they have "substantial business activities in the territory of the Party."[10] This privilege is further extended to foreign enterprises that expand operations into other NAFTA countries as long as the enterprise has substantial business activities in the NAFTA country where it originally established such operations.

NAFTA adopts a standard set of rules that allow goods containing foreign components to qualify for preferential treatment only if they undergo a "substantial transformation" within North America that results in a change of tariff classification of the product. In addition, complex value-added tests and mandatory certificates of origin attempt to ensure that firms not headquartered in North America have established true operations within the NAFTA zone. Additional requirements that products receiving reduced tariff duties through NAFTA not possess key components sourced abroad further encourages external firms to locate a greater proportion of their production process in North America.

These relatively strict rules of origin reward companies for using North American parts and labor, the incentive for which will increase as duties within NAFTA are phased out over the next few years for the majority of products. More Japanese and European firms with a North American presence can be expected to source raw materials and intermediate goods within the NAFTA area to qualify for the preferential treatment associated with NAFTA content specifications.

Increased domestic sourcing by foreign producers in North America should also encourage increased sales of intermediate goods in all three countries. This should particularly benefit the United States, which is predominant in intermediate products such as electronic equipment and machine tools.

What will NAFTA mean for the future of FDIUS? Two factors that might give us a better sense of general direction can be culled from the movement toward a single market occasioned by the NAFTA. The first is an aggregate increase in total direct investment from non-North American sources. The second is a reduction in incentives for Japanese or European investors to locate in Mexico or Canada to service the U.S. market. Both should have largely positive effects on FDIUS.

A natural and logical reaction of outsiders to the organization of a large and potentially lucrative new market is to attempt to attain greater access to it. The creation and consolidation of the European single market certainly had this effect, and the result was a significant increase in direct investment by U.S. and Japanese firms in Europe. Between 1983 and 1989, foreign direct investment in Europe from

Japan and the United States grew at approximately 30 percent per annum.[11]

While it is difficult to measure how much of this increment can be directly attributed to the anticipation of the single market, harmonization of standards, expanded economies of scale, and avoidance of anticipated common external trade barriers clearly motivated U.S. and Japanese investors to increase their direct investment in Europe. Although the global economy is now much different from that of the late 1980s, and NAFTA is nowhere near as advanced in the direction of a single market as the EU, comparable factors in the NAFTA may similarly be expected to lead to some aggregate increase in external direct investment in North America. As Table 3.3 illustrates, between 1985 and 1989 inflows of FDI into the EC(12) grew fivefold.[12]

The Japanese, in particular, stepped up their investment activity. In 1980 there were 123 Japanese-owned production units in the EC; by 1989 there were 414, and 100 planned subsequent investments.[13] From 1986 to 1990 in particular, annual inflows of Japanese direct investment increased sharply (see Table 3.4). Despite recent declines in investment and a generally cautious attitude, Japanese investors have been attracted by the simplified customs procedures, expanded market for producers, and decreased costs of distribution that they see as likely to emanate from the single market in Europe.

Table 3.3
FDI Inflows to EC (billions of ECU)

1985	05.7	1988	16.1
1986	07.1	1989	27.6
1987	12.2		

Source: *Eurostats*, 1993, p. 57.

Table 3.4
FDI Flows from Japan to the EC (millions of ECU)

1986	2,792	1989	8,846
1987	3,113	1990	8,659
1988	4,889	1991	6,435

Source: *Eurostats*, 1993, p. 57.

While some enhanced external investment can be expected from the single market characteristics of NAFTA, the allocation of that investment among NAFTA members could well be quite different from the European experience, owing to the disproportionate size and importance of the U.S. market in North America. There is also a much wider gap in development between Mexico and the United States than exists between any of the European member states.

An important aspect of U.S. and Japanese investment in Europe has been the use of less-developed member nations as export platforms to the rest of the European market. Over the course of the 1980s, Spain and Portugal, two less-developed members of the EU, became recipients of investment as "manufacturing platforms" from which Japanese and American producers gained cheaper access to the single market. Japanese and U.S. firms found it attractive to locate in areas such as these because of low production costs, the promise of relatively good infrastructure, government incentives, and, especially, duty-free access to the rest of the European market. As a consequence, consolidation of the single market in Europe appears to have acted as a spur to the use of less-developed areas as internal "export" platforms for servicing more developed, and hence higher-cost, areas of the single market.

Within North America, movement toward a single market is more likely to enhance the intrinsic advantages of the U.S. market for external investors by eliminating artificial incentives for European or Japanese firms to locate in Canada or in Mexico to service the much larger U.S. market. The United States has approximately 90 percent of the GNP of the North American market, and its GNP per capita is more than ten times that of Mexico. In contrast, German GNP is no more than 30 percent of the EU total, and German per capita GNP is about five times that of Greece. The structural disparity in market size and development among the members of the European market is much less than it is within NAFTA, and the gap in infrastructure and productivity among the members of the European Union is much less wide than it is between the United States and Mexico.

The issue of "export platforms" is an important one when viewing the impact of NAFTA on direct investment flows into the United States and is closely linked to the issue of why a manufacturer may choose to locate in one country for purposes of servicing the market in another.

Various mechanisms or programs to induce manufacturers are used by host governments to position their country as a platform for export to another country. Most are familiar tools of investment promotion, including tax holidays, foreign exchange concessions, easy terms of credit, and regulatory concessions in regards to such things as local labor laws and procurement methods. Although they are not entirely eliminated, the intent of the NAFTA is clearly to reduce export platform incentives as North America moves toward a single market. The size and wealth of the U.S. market should then draw a greater share of external investment.

For example, implementation of the forerunner to NAFTA, the Canada-U.S. FTA, was expected to encourage manufacturing investment in both countries on the part of non-FTA members in order to take advantage of the ability to produce in one country and export duty-free to the other, so long as origin requirements were met. Yet the FTA seems to have benefited the United States to a greater extent. Ottawa offered numerous export subsidies and other measures, such as customs duty remissions in the auto industry, designed to attract foreign direct investment aimed ultimately at the larger, more attractive U.S. market. Reduction in such activities by the FTA made investing in Canada less attractive as an export platform for production destined for the U.S. market and made it more attractive for the Asian transplants to locate directly in the United States.

During the 1980s, foreign auto manufacturers (primarily Japanese) made substantial direct investments in North America. Japanese firms were motivated primarily by a desire to circumvent potential imposed or "voluntary" export quotas resulting from increasing pressure by Detroit on Washington policymakers, as well as to reduce the uncertainties associated with fluctuating exchange rates.

The United States was the recipient of 80 percent of all transplant investment during this period. However, Canada was successful in attracting several large Asian manufacturers, including Honda (which invested $400 million in production facilities), Toyota ($400 million), the GM-Suzuki joint venture, CAMI ($500 million) and Hyundai ($325 million) largely by touting the ability to service the greater North American auto market from a Canadian location, so long as the transplants adhered to the domestic content requirements of the existing U.S.-Canada Auto Pact.[14] Although Canada could certainly boast of a highly skilled workforce, perhaps the major attraction for transplant Asian automakers of direct investment in Canada was Ottawa's effort to provide transplant manufacturers various duty remission and drawback programs on material brought into the country for purposes of producing exportable goods. These duty-free inducements were presumed to be particularly important to Honda, which earmarked 80 percent of its Canadian output for export to the United States, as well as Toyota, which sent 70 percent of its production to the American northeast and central regions.[15]

The elimination of Canada's favorable customs regulations ultimately benefited the United States in regard to attracting auto-related FDI. As a result of the FTA, the benefits to being located closer to the vast number of U.S. consumers (for example, lower transportation and shipping costs) could no longer be offset by the financial advantage gained by lowering production costs through the reduction in Canadian import duties.

While the United States and Canada remained the focus of auto-related investment projects during this period, Ford announced a $500 million investment to construct an assembly plant in Hermosillo, Mexico, with an original annual production target of 130,000 cars, of which 80 percent would be for the export to the United States.

Ford had been in business in Mexico since 1925, primarily assembling cars for the Mexican market with parts imported from the United States. What caused Ford to increase its investment in Mexico at a time when the major auto investment activity appeared to be centered in the United States and Canada? The decision to manufacture autos for export to the United States was driven by a number of factors. Most notable was a 1983 Mexican decree which required the five foreign car companies operating in the country to produce for export—in an effort to end the companies' negative drag on Mexico's trade balance—as a condition of being allowed to continue producing in Mexico.[16] Performance requirements such as these are being phased out by NAFTA. There should thus be a reduced incentive for external investors to locate in Mexico to service the United States and a greater incentive to locate in the United States directly.

Of course, other factors will also be at work which will have the effect of encouraging external investors to locate in Mexico. As conceded by NAFTA proponents during the debate, some jobs will be lost as certain investments are made in Mexico rather than the United States.

If closer economic integration realigns production more closely along comparative advantage lines, then NAFTA should encourage Japanese and European investors to locate in Mexico rather than the United States, primarily in unionized, low-skill manufacturing sectors such as auto parts and consumer electronics assembly.[17] Other beneficiaries of such investment in the manufacturing sector in Mexico can be expected to include food, beverages, and tobacco, steel products, machinery and equipment, and chemicals.

The growth in Mexico's exports that coincided with President Salinas' opening to the world economy gives perhaps the best indication of where Mexico's comparative advantage lies and where it is most likely to attract FDI. Automobiles and transport equipment exports increased from 7.3 percent of total exports in 1985 to 24.3 percent in 1993. Chemical products rose from 3.1 percent to 7.0 percent over the same period and electric and electronic equipment grew from 0.8 percent to 5.7 percent of total exports.[18]

One example already developing is consumer electronics. After initial hesitation during the NAFTA debate, Japanese television manufacturers are now shifting the production of key components for color television sets from Southeast Asia to Mexico. Toshiba will consolidate the manufacture of television chassis for the North American market in Mexico by September 1995, and Hitachi plans to move its chassis production from Malaysia to Mexico. Labor costs and productivity are comparable, but these companies are looking ahead to the year 2000, when tarriffs will increase for certain television components imported from outside NAFTA.

Along with the other economic reforms prompted by President Salinas, NAFTA should have the effect of increasing economic growth rates in Mexico and thus make the Mexican market more attractive, which should also serve to draw Japanese and European investors. The Mexican motor vehicle market, for example, is currently projected to grow from 600,000 cars and trucks to over 1 million by the end of the 1990s. Honda Motor Company has announced that it will begin construction of a 250,000-square-foot plant to assemble cars in El Salto, near Guadalajara. Mercedes-Benz has begun assembling cars and buses, and Toyota is expected to invest in Mexico soon for purposes of servicing this market.[19]

On balance, the preliminary indications are that the movement toward a single market occasioned by the NAFTA will have largely beneficial effects on direct investment by nonparties in the United States. The European experience indicates that movement toward a single market is likely to lead to more direct investment by external parties to enhance their overall investment in North America so as to avoid trade restrictions and to exploit the emerging North American single market.

In addition, NAFTA, by leading toward a single market in North America, can be expected to remove artificial barriers and incentives for external investors to locate elsewhere in order to service the U.S. market. Except in sectors where Mexico has a long-term comparative advantage or where internal growth gives the Mexican market inherent advantages, with artificial incentives toward export platforms such as Canadian duty remission programs and Mexican performance requirements reduced or eliminated, primary factors for investment decisions such as infrastructure, proximity to markets, and productivity of the work force should win out and help direct even more external investment to the United States.

These, of course, are only very preliminary indications. Even so, since NAFTA's approval, *Business Week* reports a new wave of Japanese investment in the United States that is at least partially attributable to NAFTA. Toyota has announced a $900 million expansion of its Georgetown, Kentucky, plant to increase local content by raising engine production and building a new model called the Avalon. Ricoh will invest $30 million to start making thermal paper products near Atlanta, so that it can be closer to its customers in the huge U.S. market, and NEC is putting $50 million into its Roseville, California, plant to make advanced 64-megabit memory chips.

Certainly, trade frictions, a stronger yen, and more rapid U.S. economic growth are also motivating factors, along with NAFTA. Nevertheless, FDIUS is now clearly a significant factor in the U.S. economy, and early indications are that the movement toward a single market in North America can be expected to enhance its importance in the years to come.

NOTES

1. In its most basic form, FDI is defined as an investment that is made to acquire a long-term interest in a business operating outside of the investor's

home country, in which the investor seeks to exercise a managerial voice over the acquired firm. Such firms are considered to be affiliates of the foreign firm. They differ from portfolio investments, which are made without prospect of exercising any managerial voice.

2. Kenneth J. Borghese, "Developments and Trends in Foreign Direct Investment in the United States," in U.S. Department of Commerce, *Foreign Direct Investment in the United States: An Update* (Washington, D.C.: 1993), p. 19.

3. Michael J. Twomey, *Multinational Corporations and the North American Free Trade Agreement*, (Westport, Conn.: Praeger, 1993), pp. 68, 69.

4. U.S. Department of Commerce, *Foreign Direct Investment in the United States*, p. 27; and Twomey, *Multinational Corporations*, p. 68.

5. Steve D. Bezirganian, "U.S. Affiliates of Foreign Companies: Operations in 1991," *Survey of Current Business*, May 1993, pp. 94, 96.

6. Ibid., p. 97.

7. U.S. Department of Commerce, Foreign Direct Investment in the United States, p. 56.

8. Bill Clinton, "NAFTA: Embracing Change," *U.S. Department of State Dispatch* 4, no. 37 (1993): 623.

9. Gary Clyde Hufbauer and Jeffrey J. Schott, "Trade Rules and New Issues," in Hufbauer and Schott, eds., *NAFTA: An Assessment* (Washington, D.C.: Institute for International Economics, 1993), p. 82.

10. Ibid.

11. *Euromoney*, May 11, p. 56.

12. Commission of the European Communities, *Panorama of EC Industry 93* (Brussels: EC, 1993), p. 57.

13. Jonathan Morris, ed., *Japan and the Global Economy: Issues and Trends in the 1990s* (London: Routledge, 1991), p. 196.

14. In order to avoid the 2.5 percent duty on cars and the 25 percent duty on trucks manufactured in Canada for export to the United States, the vehicles had to meet a 50 percent North American content rule. See *Ward's Auto World* 28, no. 1 (January 1992): 29, for data on the amount of Asian transplant investment in Canada.

15. Ibid.

16. The five companies were Ford, GM, Chrysler, VW, and Nissan.

17. Twomey, *Multinational Corporations.*

18. *The Mexican Economy 1994* (Mexico, D.F.: Banco de Mexico, 1994), p. 268.

19. *Wall Street Journal*, May 10, 1994.

PART II

POLICY OPTIONS AND ENHANCED INTERDEPENDENCE

4

When Building North America, Deepen Before Widening

Charles F. Doran

Regional trade groupings must learn to crawl before they walk. If the final objective of closer interdependence and greater market efficiency is to be obtained, certain tasks necessarily precede others.[1] This is true regardless of the type of regional trade grouping. In the case of NAFTA, as much deepening as is possible ought to precede widening, so that the objective of a more productive North American economy can eventuate.

Two political factors make this advice problematic, however. First, early widening is very seductive and politically rather easy to achieve for the original members of the trade area or other grouping. All the original members must do is wait for a suitable candidate. The threat of trade and investment diversion will quickly force other regional actors to contemplate joining the original trade area or market. Moreover, the benefits are rather immediate, thus adding to the attraction. Economies of scale will surely result, and the gains to trade from widening can be impressive. Creation of a larger market in which the division of labor can work itself out more fully rewards the ease of widening with a quick economic and political payoff.

Second, the process known as deepening, the effort to generate greater policy harmonization, is always a more painful process for the founders of the trade area. They either must revisit old issues of disagreement, or they must push forward with new initiatives that may be equally difficult to negotiate. Sometimes policy harmonization breaks entirely new ground conceptually and in bargaining terms. This is the most difficult form of deepening. Of course the gains to trade here, and the consequent market efficiencies, can be truly gigantic. Unfortunately, the benefits may not be as immediate as in the case of widening, and the political costs may come early.

Yet a more deep-seated political factor underlies the advice to deepen before widening. The argument made in this chapter is that for political reasons of internal bargaining and consensus building, unless deepening proceeds first, widening may be the only option. The act of widening may itself preclude some types of deepening. Access of new members with different political, economic, social, and even cultural agendas may generate so much diversity and conflict that deepening in the future becomes moot. Widening cancels out the chance for closer policy harmonization. Under these circumstances, widening thus becomes the only future option.

If the architects of a trade grouping want both widening and deepening, that is in fact possible. But such dual-process integration is likely only if deepening takes place first. Then later candidates for accession will not be tempted to veto deepening. Instead, they will accept the more refined trade area as a complete package, with deepening intact. Such an enlightened strategy for both deepening and widening ensures that an optimal outcome regarding increased integration will occur. When deepening precedes widening, a more efficient trade area is likely to ensue with respect to change on both strategic dimensions. The architects of trade and investment liberalization will find that they are able to escape the trap of having to give up one set of economic benefits.

EFFECTS OF `WIDENING' VERSUS `DEEPENING'

Speaking in this matter virtually for all three NAFTA governments, Canada's Trade Minister Roy McLaren says, "Canada will do what it can to facilitate the broadening, as well as deepening, of the Agreement."[2] Widening versus deepening within NAFTA, however, takes on special gravity today. The arrangement is at a decision threshold.

Widening and deepening promote market efficiency: Widening, by increasing the size of the market area, and thereby providing greater economies of scale to production; Deepening, by eliminating more internal barriers to trade of a policy sort that inhibit the unfettered movement of goods and services within the trade area. Thus, on prima facie grounds, widening and deepening are both desirable, especially where the trade benefits generated create welfare rather than divert it from other trading partners. Likewise, both widening and deepening create new opportunities for domestic and foreign investment. Where this new investment is genuinely new, rather than attracted away from other trading partners, the respective processes are innovative and positive for the world trading system as well as for North America.

Three temporal possibilities exist. First, NAFTA could choose to widen first by adding new members.[3] The current favorite is Chile, because, of all the possible candidates, its economy seems to be most open and readily adaptable to NAFTA norms. Second, NAFTA could choose to deepen first by bringing standards, tax policies, and other programs of subsidy and investment policy more closely in line. Somewhat ironically, this is what the special panels on labor standards and on the environment are supposed to do, although their presence may have the opposite result—interference with greater trade efficiency. Third, NAFTA could attempt to widen and deepen at the same time. This is, in practice, what the European Union is attempting.

Insofar as neither widening nor deepening precludes the other from making progress, and insofar as the benefit of each is equal and the political feasibility of each is similar (financial and political costs of implementation are equal), there is no reason to choose among the three strategies. Whatever comes first on the agenda is satisfactory. However, if widening provides greater benefits to the original members than deepening, it may take priority. Likewise, if the cost of implementation of widening or deepening is higher, this fact alone may determine the order of initiation. Finally, and most compellingly, if either widening or deepening in effect precludes the other, or substantially postpones the interval in which the other can be introduced, then this factor must weigh heavily on the choice of temporal ordering.

As noted, the European Union seems to be proceeding under the assumption that the last set of conditions holds, that there is no particular temporal order that is advantageous over any other.[4] Some widening is initiated, then some deepening, and so on, in pragmatic fashion. The original Common Market's eight members seem content with this approach.

However, I propose quite a different strategy. The proposition I make here is that, despite some advantages peculiar to the type of advanced common market enjoyed by the Europeans (their elaborate institutions manage the shock of change), the temporal order of widening versus deepening does matter very much. Following this proposition is a hypothesis drawn from theoretical argument about which should proceed first, widening or deepening, and with what consequence for future economic interdependence and integration.

Proposition I: The temporal sequence in which widening occurs relative to deepening is critical to the fullest development of market efficiencies within a regional trade grouping.

Hypothesis I: All other things being equal, deepening ought to proceed before widening, so as to obtain the fullest economic benefits from a regional trade grouping.

This proposition and hypothesis contain a logic that is as follows. Widening versus deepening does matter in terms of which goes first because some things are precluded when the wrong choice is made. Other things are needlessly postponed by making the wrong choice. The basic argument is this: If the objective is to create a regional community in which the greatest market efficiencies prevail, members ought to proceed with deepening as expeditiously as possible. Only then should the original members seek to widen the participation. This is not an argument against widening. It is an argument against widening before the necessary deepening has taken place.

In essence, the proposition is that each country possesses a given type of industrial structure. When governments come together to form a regional trade grouping, they cement a new set of commercial and trade relations that corresponds to their own indigenous industrial structures.[5] When new governments are added to the grouping, new industrial structures must be made to conform to the original industrial structure. But this requires painful and difficult change. Political resistance is inevitable. It is this political resistance that not only slows down accommodation but actually precludes certain kinds of initiatives. If the desire is to have a tightly integrated economic market maximizing efficiency among the original members, then the members must obtain this degree of integration first, in a fashion that corresponds to their own industrial makeup.

The hypothesis is that when new members join a trade grouping, they add structural, political, and cultural diversity. All of this is enriching, and potentially quite beneficial to economic specialization. Unfortunately, this additional diversity is also likely to introduce conflict into bargaining relationships. The greater the diversity (the greater the number of states involved), the more difficult it is to obtain agreement about a given level of trade liberalization. A greater amount of diversity is likely to lead to a common denominator of agreement that is more shallow than with a lesser amount of diversity, everything else being equal.

According to this hypothesis, then, deepening among the original members ought to come first. Then other members can join the trade grouping, their participation being phased in. But very important, because they join later, the new members will not be in a position to veto progress toward deepening. Widening will not get in the way of deepening. Conversely, if widening takes place first, the greater diversity in the trade grouping is likely to lead to an erosion of momentum for deepening. This is true because so many compromises must be made, across so many issues, as a result of the enormous structural, political, and cultural diversity that the larger trade grouping encompasses.

On the other hand, if deepening proceeds first, then widening can take place on the basis of liberalization within an industrial, trading, and investment framework that is ambitious and far-reaching. Within that framework, liberalization will not be as much hostage to erosion by newer members who seek to limit progress toward deepening. The latter will obtain a firm target for admission. They will know the types of changes they will need to make in order to qualify. They can seek some extensions, and perhaps even a few small exemptions, but fundamentally they will be required to meet the ambitious standards of liberalization set by the original members.

A trade area based on advanced liberalization of trade, investment, and other rules that impinge on the economy will be much more of a community, and will be much more market efficient, than a looser, more diverse trade grouping of larger size that is still groping for a common denominator of progressive liberalization and standardization. Optimally, therefore, deepening ought to precede widening. Widening is certainly desirable, but not at the price of greater deepening, which is in fact the price the original members will pay when conflict over structures or standards of efficiency, arising from increased diversity, begins to undermine negotiation and agreement.

Let us now look at the European Community to see how this proposition and hypothesis are borne out. The original eight members of the Common Market had comparatively similar industrial structures, per capita incomes, political regimes, and cultural outlooks. They also had a common vision of where they wanted to go. As new members have been added, diversity has strained the communality of purpose. Britain, for example, questions the common monetary policy and use of a single currency. Spain, Portugal, and Greece have agricultural economies that are putting pressure on the common agricultural policy. Admission of Poland, the Czech Republic, and Slovakia would put stress on the European Union in terms of subsidies and regional development programs. Even Switzerland, with a sophisticated financial and manufacturing base, would, as a member, drag the European Union in another direction, not only in these areas of economic emphasis but also in terms of agriculture, since among the advanced industrial countries Switzerland's subsidies are highest.

Europe responds by offering two strategies. First, it proposes phased-in entry of countries to reach the common standard (a multi-speed Europe). Second, it proposes "tiered" levels of integration, with the upper tier going furthest toward a common monetary policy, a common currency, and perhaps common political structures. That response contains at least two flaws of argument, however.

First, the purpose of reducing trade impediments is to reduce them, not to create new ones that may be less transparent, less quantifiable, and more complex. Multiple speeds and tiers are satisfactory if they are temporary. But if they become permanent aspects of the trade and investment environment, as many of these arrangements are likely to do, then "interim" devices to bridge so many different economic structures are likely to be a remedy worse than the original disease of simple protectionism.

Second, the real problem is more subtle. Once diversity is added to the community through widening, the new members are virtually equal with the original members. The newer members may veto efforts to deepen liberalization through policy harmonization. Such deepening may indeed be harder for them to implement than for the original members. Whether that is true, the tendency to want a "shallower" market, or at any rate a different market, may undermine future efforts to deepen. It may not be that the new members do not want to liberalize further. The problem may only be that they want to move in another direction, thus complicating the decision-making and ultimately causing the liberalization effort to stall. Fearful of this result, Europe is reluctant to accept Muslim Turkey into the European Union, even though Turkey is a democracy and has long been a very responsible member of NATO.

Politics will not help here. To the contrary, on political grounds the original members of the European Community are hard-pressed not to admit governments from Eastern Europe as well as from all of Europe. Not to admit looks discriminatory. Moreover, there is a great incentive to widen rather than to deepen because the "quick fix" obtained from a larger market and economies of scale is hard to resist. Widening is politically easier for the original members to adjust to than deepening, because the burden of adjustment is placed on the newer members, not the increasingly sizable older trading area. Politically, the easy thing to do in a trade group is to widen rather than to deepen, even if this process ultimately leads to stagnation in the overall process of liberalization.

This argument leads to a second hypothesis about the relationship between deepening and widening.

Hypothesis II: When they proceed with widening prematurely, trade groups reach diminishing marginal returns in terms of deepening.

The objective is to obtain the maximum efficiencies from both deepening and widening. Both occur across a long, dynamic frontier of change. To benefit the most from the liberalization strategy, deepening ought to proceed as far and as fast as possible among the original signatories to the trade arrangement before adding new members. At the very least, the new members must be examined not just on their capacity to meet the terms of an existing agreement. They must also meet the terms of future extensions of the agreement that will provide benefits from policy harmonization and standardization. Ascertaining willingness and capacity here may prove much more challenging, especially since governments are inevitably testing a "hypothetical," that is, a hypothetical form of deeper trade, investment, and policy liberalization to be initiated sometime in the future.

European integration is likely to pay a high price for accepting the "easy way out" in terms of further liberalization. By adding many new members before moving further and faster to coalesce the original signatories to the Rome Treaties, they have probably destroyed the opportunity to reach their original objective of building a supra-national entity. They have added so much diversity and internal conflict that progress toward tighter political integration, even tighter economic integration of the sort involved in a single monetary policy, is now extraordinarily difficult. Few members have the will to say no to new entrants, but few new entrants seem reluctant to say no to real progress toward a truly united Europe.

In at least one way, the European Union has an advantage that other regions may not share. It possesses a highly institutionalized community designed in part to offset the conflict that emerges because of heterogeneity and diversity. North America will not enjoy this buffer, since its objective is not to move toward political integration.[6] North America is not only suspicious of the loss of sovereignty entailed in the creation of supranational institutions, but it is suspicious of the financial cost, and of the rigidity imposed by supranationality. But without the institutions to mitigate conflict among the members over future liberalization, the prospect for deepening inside a very large regional trade group is even more remote.

These arguments are multifold compelling where, as in North America, the clash between devolution and evolution is so unsettled. The wrong choice could send the North American community spiralling down the devolutionary path with little integration economically and a considerable potential for societal fragmentation.[7]

IMPLICATIONS FOR CHOICE WITH RESPECT TO DEEPENING IN NORTH AMERICA

One large conclusion emerges from this discussion: "Deepen before you widen." Deepen according to a conception of North American society and of North American community that will help cope with the problems facing this region in the twenty-first century.[8] Deepen also in terms of what will strengthen competitiveness through the creation of a market that is as efficient as any in the global system. But bear in mind that deepening is a dynamic process in the sense that the international standard is continually moving forward. The task of efficiency creation is never complete. By devising strategy in advance, the goal ought to be to remain "ahead of the curve" globally.

Attract other states to the regional trade area, but do so on the basis of having to meet as high a standard of regional market efficiency as is possible. Full membership is the eventual goal for all constituent states, although "phased-in participation" is surely acceptable. But the new members should not be allowed to hold the process of deepening hostage, as they surely will if they are admitted prematurely. All of this is even more valid where the trade area would like to avoid creating supranational institutions. These institutions serve to regulate and to reduce conflict during the deepening process, and after. In the absence of them, the task of policy harmonization is difficult enough without having to face the hostility of latecomers to the prospect of generating a market that is truly efficient and free of inhibitors to trade and investment mobility.

Deepening comes in two forms. Innovative deepening "breaks new ground" within the trade area in terms of policy harmonization and the installation of new common standards. It establishes priorities for additional liberalization, a timetable for such advancement, and tactics for how to proceed. Remedial deepening is the type that many analysts have forgotten because they have assumed that the effort to create a trade area is a one-step enterprise. Remedial deepening is necessary to clear away the "underbrush" that grows up after the "tall timber" of tariff protectionism has been removed. Remedial deepening requires special tools.

Innovative deepening ought to use as a model the openness that exists in any well-run market economy. By comparing the present relations among the member states in NAFTA, for example, with the economic conditions that exist inside Germany, Britain, or the United States, the program for innovative deepening becomes clear. Standards that differ regarding product safety, labeling, measurement, and advertising must not be allowed to act as purposeful inhibitors to the movement of goods and services. Environmental, health, and tax policies should, insofar as possible, eliminate distortive characteristics that restrict trade and commerce. Such policies are often cherished by a polity and regarded as indispensable.

Where protective policies are regarded as sacred cows, there is likely to be little progress. Canada has its protection of the "cultural industries." The United States for good reasons guards "national security concerns." Both Canada and the United States are protective regarding immigration. Mexico has particular sensitivity toward its petroleum sector and, as we are likely to see, toward parts of its agricultural sector.[9] Progress toward uniformization of policy treatment in these areas is possible but not easy.

A key dilemma with innovative deepening is that the objective is surely to reduce policy distortion that restricts the movement of goods and services. But the objective is also to retain a high quality of performance and service in each area. Hence Canada does not want a health system that is less than universal. The United States does not want a health system that rations care. Mexico does not want to be held to a standard of care which a country with its per capita income cannot underwrite financially. Each of these priorities is apparently as valid for the society as market efficiency itself. Together these priorities are so opposed that health care will probably remain a country-specific program.

Standards of purity and of salubriousness must not be harmonized by dilution, that is, by reducing them to the lowest common denominator. An effort must be made to move toward the highest standards within the trade area. Of course this challenges the ability of the poorer member, or the member that has a weaker history of implementing and enforcing standards. If goods and services are to move freely back and forth across borders, these tasks of enhancing standards must be given early attention.

Yet without conscious coordination of policy within a trade area, chaos will result. When Canada attempted to establish a "sin tax" on cigarettes and liquor that was higher than that imposed in the United States, the result was predictable. Smuggling flourished. Coordination of excise taxes ought to be explicit, if it is not already implicit, across borders within the trade area.

In short, everything from movement toward the metric system of measurement, to the elimination of inconsistencies and distortions associated with services such as insurance and banking, will do much to strengthen and open the respective national segments of the unified trade area. The North American trade area ought to appoint a high commission of advisers to identify and recommend standards and policies ripe for such harmonization.

Remedial deepening is not so familiar a concept. The basic notion is that remedial deepening must remove all of the nontariff barriers that have been set up to stop trade and investment in the aftermath of the elimination of tariffs. Nontariff barriers are less transparent, and in some cases more protective, than the original tariffs.[10] Yet without remedial deepening these new barriers to cross-border trade and investment will merely replace the old barriers, yet in a more invidious way.

Examples abound. In the aftermath of NAFTA, the U.S. steel industry filed a raft of anti-dumping cases. Mexico imposed its own anti-dumping duties, up to 79 percent, which the U.S. industry did not oppose, since it was doing the same thing. Inspections are a common way of slowing down trade or, in the case of perishables, eliminating trade. The United States, after NAFTA, applies an inspection fee of $30 a truckload of lumber for "sanitary certificates." Mexico "inspects" even kiln-dried wood already heated to 280°F., and charges $32 to "validate" the certificates. Some duties are outright challenges to NAFTA. In May 1994 the United States raised anti-dumping duties on Mexican cement from 43 percent to 60 percent.

The principal industries affected by the rebellion against NAFTA are cement, lumber, meat, steel, and dairy. But more are likely to follow, such as toys and textiles. Techniques include anti-dumping duties, inspections, and new regulations. When the new labor safety, environmental, and health standards are fully registered, much of the benefit of NAFTA may disappear. Labeling restrictions alone can halt much trade in goods because the prohibition can be total.

Perhaps the biggest problem associated with the new rules, rules that remedial deepening must rethink, is the paperwork that is required on both sides of the border. Much of this is attributable to "rules-of-origin" concerns about transshipping, and was fully predicted before NAFTA came into effect. If this paper burden for government and business becomes unbearable, Canada, the United States, and Mexico will need to reconsider establishing a common market instead of a free-trade area, so as to minimize rules-of-origin procedures necessitated by the existence of different tariffs for each member country.

In sum, the planners of a free trade area must not rely solely on innovative deepening to expand the benefits of freer trade and investment in the future. They must also establish a program of remedial deepening at the time the agreement is signed, so as to roll back the nontariff onslaught that surely will follow tariff reduction. Otherwise, analysts and businessmen will be judging the merits of a trade liberalization agreement that in very few aspects conforms to the letter of the original terms.

Moreover, to add new members to an agreement when deepening has barely begun in the old agreement, and when remedial problems have not yet been adequately handled, is to add so much diversity and potential conflict to the liberalization effort that no one will really know what anyone else in the agreement is offering or expecting. Just as simplicity in any of these trade liberalization agreements is the best way to avoid future abuse of the agreement, so clearly thought-out innovative and remedial deepening is the best way to create a market that yields results in terms of greater efficiency at home.[11] This then becomes the kind of trade area others can most usefully join and, ultimately, will determine whether North America as a region evolves or devolves.

A CLASH OF VALUES: EFFICIENCY VERSUS SOVEREIGNTY

At the end of the eighteenth century, "Great Britain was the largest free-trade area in the Western World," according to Arnold Toynbee, "a fact which goes far to explain why it was in Great Britain and not elsewhere that the Industrial Revolution began.[12] The American colonies in 1788 "abolished all commercial barriers between the States and created what was to become by natural expansion the largest free-trade area, and by direct consequence the mightiest industrialized community, in the world today."[13] Modern France, Italy, and Germany likewise developed through the elimination of trade barriers. The European Union now supplants the European nation-state as the preferred unit of trade and commercial rationalization. ASEAN is the prototype for regional trade liberalization in Asia. Is it any wonder that the United States, Mexico, and Canada overwhelmingly approved NAFTA as the vehicle to push North American economic growth and prosperity into the twenty-first century?

Despite strong approval for NAFTA, the trade-off is large between political sovereignty and efficiency, that is, between what the individual member-states want and what trade areas are able to promise. In exploring the widening versus deepening debate, this chapter is assessing a value trade-off.

Although not always regarded that way, political sovereignty and market efficiency are at odds. Attitudes toward this dichotomy seem to differ in Europe and in North America. Political sovereignty appears to be more strongly cherished by each of the three North American countries than by Holland, Italy, Germany, or even France. The corresponding cost is a somewhat diminished potential for regional market efficiency accomplished through reduction of trade and commercial barriers. By predisposition, Europe has been willing to go further and faster in terms of regional economic integration than North America.

Europe of course has a greater history of intra-regional conflict than North America, especially recent and monumental conflict exemplified by the two world wars. Political integration in Europe is designed to preclude such war in the future. The civil war in Bosnia in the aftermath of the breakup of the Soviet empire only heightens awareness of this goal of a unified Europe that would bury the violent past. European political integration received impetus as well from the feeling of all European states that the world had grown up around them and had dwarfed them. Continent-sized states now dominated the international system. Thus European political integration was conceived as a way for Europe to hold its own on the world stage.

None of this preoccupies North Americans. Neither Canadians nor Mexicans seem to dream of a world role beyond their present means, certainly not an attempt to restore past dreams of empire and a global reach. The United States, despite awareness of a decline in relative power, does not worry much about its ability to compete globally for influence. Bloody wars have occurred in the North American region, but the last was the American Civil War almost a century and a half ago. Nobody believes such a thing could happen again. Hence there is little desire to create a prophylactic through regional political integration to avert something, the revival of warfare, that is not likely to happen again in North America. North Americans do not face the same problems, or share the same fears, as Europeans; hence those living in North America are not trying to build a regional political superstructure. Indeed, the opposite is the case. North Americans want the fruits of regional economic integration without having to pay the costs of sovereignty forgone.

But this task of extracting the benefits of greater market efficiency, without paying the costs in terms of giving up some sovereignty, is a difficult exercise. Political institutions and economic institutions are of course far from identical. With the emergence of the multinational corporation that now handles perhaps two-thirds of total world trade, this disparity between political and economic institutions is even wider than before. But the nation-state seeks to control its own destiny. A large part of that destiny is the welfare interest of its citizens. For the most part, North American governments still believe that they can, and do, control the economic welfare of their citizenry. These governments do not deny the existence of interdependence. But neither do they stake their very survival on that interdependence. Sovereignty-transferring organizations such as GATT, NAFTA, and the U.S.-Canada Free Trade Agreement are always regarded as quasi-threats to the governability of the state even as these agreements promise increased prosperity, perhaps nowhere else as attainable in policy terms.

The clash between the values of independence and prosperity is currently starkest in the two trends of societal change within North America, evolution versus devolution. One is the trend toward greater centralization of institutions, including the concentration of power at the federal level. The other is the trend toward decentralization of functions and responsibilities, including the localization of power at the subnation-state level, or in some cases the potential fragmentation of the nation-state itself. Evolution and devolution are perpetually at odds in all regions and in all periods of history. But in North America the tension is currently quite noteworthy.

REGIONAL EVOLUTION VERSUS DEVOLUTION

On the one hand, the evolutionary trend is broadly evident. Since the administrations of Franklin D. Roosevelt in the United States, the federal government has taken on more responsibilities both for taxation and for the provision of services. It has gotten into regulation, enforcement, and the distribution of services. From civil rights enforcement to the administration of social security, the federal government has become the most visible agency of social change. Now even education and health care are on the verge of being regulated, and to some extent financed, from Washington. Mexico has always been a highly centralized polity, a situation facilitated by the monopoly control of the governing party, the PRI, for over six decades.[14] Canada, at least since the first governments of Pierre Elliott Trudeau, has self-consciously developed social programs, tax powers, and techniques of regulation that are highly centralized in Ottawa. The practice of redistributing tax dollars to the provinces on a need basis goes much further toward centralized administration than is true in the United States, despite the capacity of the provinces to determine how they wish to spend the funds. Purposeful development of multiculturalism and of bilingualism is designed to build a bridge at the federal level between the francophone and anglophone communities. A fairly rough index of how fast the federal programs in each of these polities has evolved is to look at the growth of both bureaucratic size and spending at the federal level since midcentury. Relative to the size of the state/provincial budgets and bureaucracies, which also have grown significantly, the federal pattern is even more striking.

To some extent the recent pattern of regionwide trade and commercial negotiation is just a further expansion of the trend toward the centralization of authority, even though the U.S.-Canada and the NAFTA agreements undercut the power of the national governments to some extent. Power to pursue policies of subsidy and countervail are limited in the name of greater regional market efficiency. This means that individual governments have given up some authority over these issues.

On the other hand, devolutionary trends are at least as discernible as the evolutionary, and perhaps more recent. Since the Reagan and Mulroney governments, some attempt has been made to decentralize authority over a range of social services, partly to cover a federal revenue shortfall, partly under the belief that these services would be better administered locally and that people felt closer to their local governments. In the case of Canada, this policy was purposely calculated to make Quebec feel more of a "master in its own house." In the case of Mexico, northern Mexico, with its growing wealth and industrial power, is beginning to challenge Mexico City for political leadership, following the mandates of its Conservative party and the preferences of its local elites. Perhaps the epitome of this devolutionary political trend is the visibility and success of the Bloc Quebecois and of the Parti Quebecois in promoting separation. Quebec's separation from Canada would establish an entirely unique level of devolutionary vigor in North America. It could become a model for separatist feeling in northern Mexico, and in the area from Texas to Southern California, causing these subfederal communities to begin to think about political estrangement as well, unlikely as this cognition seems in the twentieth century.[15]

Proponents of political devolution, however, usually tend to speak of economic evolution at the same time. That is why the trends are sometimes ambiguous to the point of being undecipherable. For example, it was Reagan and Mulroney, the proponents of limited devolution, who also sought the regional trade agreements at a time when they were quite opposed by more liberal elements in both societies. Quebec nationalists are among the strongest supporters of regional free trade. It is not too much to argue that regional free trade is the cornerstone of the Quebec separatist movement, and that without it no opportunity for serious discussion of autonomy would be possible.

The explanation for the existence of these somewhat surprising countertrends is not hard to unearth.[16] The proponents of various kinds of devolution believe that they can have the benefits of economic evolution at the same time. They believe that categories of policy may be closed off from devolutionary influence, and that the trade-off between political sovereignty and economic efficiency is bridgeable. Political sovereignty can be decentralized. Economic efficiency, through evolutionary changes, can be centralized. The nation-state can become more responsive to the concerns of the voters and, concurrently, the marketplace can become more productive through economies of scale. Devolution and evolution need not collide.

Perhaps the most probing question that faces North America today is whether this vision of devolution and evolution within state and region is logically consistent and politically manageable. Are the two trends compatible?[17]

Subsidiarity

This doctrine is something of an official strategy for the European Union. In concept it is appealing. The reason devolution and evolution do not clash, according to the principle of subsidiarity, is that they can be properly managed. Devolution of some categories of policy, at or beneath the state level, actually bolsters evolutionary movement toward the suprastate level. The principle at work is that any policy which can better be carried out at a lower administrative level is automatically entrusted to that lower level.

By this means policy remains close to the people and is more efficiently implemented. Only those policies that must be executed at the regionwide level are allowed to ascend to that level. At work is a kind of political-economic centrifuge. The "heavy" policies that should be dealt with at a lower administrative level are carried out at that level. The "lighter" policies that must be managed over a broader regional area are allowed to rise to that level. This separation process keeps regional integration lively and efficient. There is less tendency for bureaucratic overload at the top because this "centrifugal" process of separation adroitly differentiates and is ongoing.

In concept, this is an elegant solution to the problem of a clash between evolutionary and devolutionary tendencies within the integrative process. We know where delineation ought to occur and according to what principle. Subsidiarity appears to combine the best of both the evolutionary and devolutionary trends of integration. Sovereignty over what is important is not lost. Efficiency results. Yet the region-wide community has control over what it needs to make integration a success.

If ever there was a principle that sounds plausible but lacks ease and precision of application, it is the principle of subsidiarity. The problem is that almost all services, for example, could benefit from a lower level of implementation, closer to those who will use the service. Here problems enter. In order to keep the quality of the service uniform across a region, regionwide administrative procedures and bureaucracies for implementation are needed. Think of retirement benefits or social security. In order to pay for the service and maintain it at a comparatively high level of quality, funding must come from across the entire region. Think of transfer payments across the Canadian provinces or the German Länder. This process of taxation and distribution of funds is centralized so that rich regions in effect subsidize poorer regions. Centralization is unavoidable. In order to enforce standards fairly, they must have a regionwide focus. Consider the American Civil Rights Act and its enforcement, for example. Otherwise, standards in some locales will deteriorate.

In the end, the problem with subsidiarity is that scarcely a policy would not benefit in terms of efficiency, and in terms of the retention of sovereign control by the electorate, through consigning the service to a lower level of administration. However, because of offsetting difficulties of financing, administration, and enforcement, to say nothing of political resistance, scarcely a single major policy program will ever be allowed to devolve to a lower subregional authority, at least not without self-defeating strings attached by the centralized regional authority.

Evolutionary Devolution (Creative Destruction)

This approach to an amalgamation of devolutionary and evolutionary trends is likewise quite creative. Some German proponents of the "European idea" advocate evolutionary devolution. Because of the history of strong German bureaucratic centralization, the movement toward regional integration is thought to be hindered.[18] The nation-state is too strong. It is adverse to subjecting itself to the forces of supranationality. Too irresistible, the desire for sovereignty by the state prevents regional integration from moving forward.

Hence, by devolving certain responsibilities, the authority of the state is purposely undermined. This devolution of responsibility counters the centralizing tendencies of the state. By weakening the state, the regionwide community is then able to pick up these responsibilities and to administer or to enforce them on behalf of the whole community of societies (states).

This is creative destruction. What looks like devolution is in fact evolution. To ascend, the pattern of implementation must first descend. To centralize at a higher level, one must first decentralize at a lower level. To strengthen the regional community, one must first weaken the nation-state. To build sovereignty regionally, one must undercut sovereignty at the state level.

The problem with this process of evolutionary devolution is that though it may eventually increase efficiency by centralizing functions at the regionwide level, this process surely does not retain sovereignty for the nation-state. In fact, the purpose of creative destruction is to do just the opposite, namely, to limit the sovereignty of the state so that this sovereignty can later be transferred to the regionwide community. Evolutionary devolution may be used by the European Union to strengthen itself. It does not appear to be a process that any of the three North American governments would favor, because they do not want to yield sovereignty for a more centralized purpose, even if that purpose is greater economic efficiency to be shared by all.

Segmentalism

The third method of attempting to overcome the clash between evolution and devolution in North America is segmentalism. This method distinguishes between economic considerations, on the one hand, and political and cultural considerations, on the other. Segmentalism tries to create "watertight compartments" into each of which a separate set of considerations is placed. Economics and politics are "segmented," that is, they are divided and assigned to different levels of administrative authority.

Perhaps the most prominent example of segmentalism is the doctrine of "sovereignty-association" promoted by the Parti Quebecois under the late René Levesque. According to sovereignty-association, Quebec ought to secede politically from Canada while retaining many, if not all, joint economic functions. Quebec would retain the Canadian dollar as its currency. It would submit to a slightly reconstituted Canadian central bank. It would belong to a North America-wide trade area. Both the U.S.-Canada FTA and the NAFTA would extend to Quebec without alteration. Quebec in cultural and political terms would be independent. In economic terms it would be fully integrated with its primary trading and investment partners.

How plausible is this delineation of function? Apart from the matter of the political attractiveness of sovereignty-association, for Quebec, Canada, or anyone else, the technical feasibility of segmentalism merits further examination.[19] Surely independent political actors can join a trade area or common market without giving up the bulk of their autonomous political functions. That is already true for the members of the European Union and for the North American trade area. What sovereignty-association entailed was a degree of economic association between Quebec and the rest of Canada that slightly exceeds that in the present-day European Union. After all, no single monetary authority or single currency has yet been adopted inside Europe, though it has been proposed in the Maastricht treaties. So sovereignty-association, despite its ambiguity, is neither implausible administratively nor contradictory in terms of function. But one can question how stable such an arrangement would be over time.

With the European Union, a host of community institutions has been in place for decades, including the Commission, the Parliament, and a European Court. The political objective presumably is to transfer sovereignty from the state to the European Community. Yet in North America the Quebec objective would be to move sovereignty in the opposite direction, from federation to province, while leaving a fairly high degree of economic association with the federation. But what happens when there are disagreements over how joint monetary policy is determined, or whether a common exchange rate policy is advantageous? There are neither communitywide institutions in North America to assume broader administration of these economic functions, nor a mentality of supranationalism that would get the various polities through periods of intense disagreement. Very possibly, Quebec and the rest of Canada would find further derogation of economic function from the region in their respective political interests. Sovereignty would ultimately weigh more heavily than economic efficiency in the political thinking of elites.

In sum, each attempt to combine the trends of evolution and devolution has its problems. Subsidiarity, though conceptually sound, is difficult to apply in a fashion that works. Evolutionary devolution may appeal to elites in Europe, but its strategy of "creative destruction" at the state level would not find much support politically in North America. Segmentalism, including that espoused in sovereignty-association, is conceptually consistent and perhaps administratively feasible, but it lacks commitment to a communitywide outlook that would save it from breakdown in the face of the inevitable differences over policy implementation that are likely to result.

Thus the question of whether North America is likely to move in the direction of evolution or of devolution over time is still moot. The clash of perspectives is far from having been sorted out. In North America, proponents of increased market efficiency still have a long way to go to make their case to the theorist or the politician.

A REGION LIKE NO OTHER?

Perhaps North America is a region like no other. Perhaps the dominant presence of the United States solves both the dilemma of widening versus deepening and the associated problem of evolution versus devolution. According to this argument, North America is different from the European Community, for example, because the United States is so much bigger than the other members of the trade area. This dominant presence can be counted on to solve each of the foregoing quandaries, since the United States in effect will make the principal decisions.

That this argument scarcely holds in terms of the evolution versus devolution debate is surely apparent. Quebec will do what it thinks best for its own interests, regardless of the preferences of the United States or, for that matter of English Canada, which is about three times larger in economic and population terms than Quebec. At the center of the region size may affect some policy choices in the short-term, but it is not likely to determine subregional and intra-national decisions about centralization throughout the region in the long term.

Likewise, the differential size of the United States is not likely to guarantee control over outcomes with respect to deepening, especially where the widening route is chosen initially. Of course the United States has had enormous impact on the design of the initial arrangements and even upon whether such a trade arrangement would go forward at all. It is true that the United States has great veto power over the speed and direction of the integration process. But will the United States have the capacity to initiate steps toward deepening, over the heads of possibly reluctant and more numerous partners to NAFTA, in the future?

A measure of the degree to which the United States faces curbs on its decision autonomy is found in the trade dispute resolution mechanism. Despite the fact that only about 5 percent of the total trade covered by NAFTA ever is involved in a dispute proceeding, once such a proceeding is invoked, the United States is subject to the same discipline as the smaller members. In practice, this has meant that more disputes have been "won" by Canada than by the United States under the FTA, although most trade experts do not like to interpret the outcomes in win-loss sovereignty terms. In any case, the United States must abide by the same rules of trade review as its regional partners.

There is also a tendency in the United States to think that market efficiency equates with "what we have." Often that is true, because of the size and productivity of the U.S. economy. But this equation is not always true. Over time, in the midst of the give-and-take of bargaining, finding where policy convergence and market efficiency meet will be politically more difficult for the United States, internal to the polity as well as external to it within the enlarged trade area.

The United States may propose various deepening strategies, such as policy harmonization and improved standard-setting. But the other members will necessarily be asked to give their assent. The procedures may become as complicated as the voting within the European Union, or as simple as the NAFTA rules, where each state merely gives its approval. But without the buffer of supranational institutions, and set against the increasing cultural, geographic, political, and economic diversity that widening will bring, there is little confidence that the newer members, and indeed the older members like Canada, will automatically consent to a new agenda that sharply affects their capacity for societal differentiation. On many issues at least one state is likely to balk. Vetoes are easier than policy initiation. Deepening is likely more and more to become a casualty of disagreement in NAFTA, despite the ascendancy of the United States, just as such disagreement has slowed down integration within the European Union, notwithstanding close coordination of policies between France and Germany.

Canada and Mexico are already murmuring that the addition of new members will help "balance" the United States. The United States should not take umbrage over this thoroughly normal behavior of sovereign governments. But the addition of new members will be much easier to manage than the deepening of existing trade arrangements. In this, the United States should not delude itself because of the ease of past negotiation. Far from facilitating consensus, the comparative ascendancy of the United States is likely to encourage "coalitional thinking" on the part of the other members of the NAFTA. This should not induce paranoia. But political realism about what the future may hold strategically is certainly prudent.

North America is for many reasons unique. U.S. power and wealth contribute to this uniqueness. But the rules of diplomatic conduct and bargaining will not stand aside in the deepening versus widening debate, based on the rationality and good fortune that integration in North America so far has enjoyed. The simple maxim still holds: Deepen first, widen later.

A North American metaphor perhaps will sharpen the choices available. Suppose trade areas were like lakes. One choice is Lake

Erie, a nice, broad body of water. A bit murky and polluted, it is also very shallow. Lake Superior, on the other hand, is deep and clear. It is the source of most of North America's freshwater supply. North Americans, which model do you prefer regarding economic integration, Lake Erie or Lake Superior?

NOTES

1. This thesis challenges contemporary theoretical argument regarding economic integration, in part because it stems from political as well as economic observation. Therefore the thesis will be regarded by some as controversial. For the more traditional argument see Paul Robson, *The Economics of International Integration,* 2nd ed. (London: Allen and Unwin, 1984); and Bela Balassa, *The Theory of Economic Integration* (London: Allen and Unwin, 1962). An appreciation of the blend of the political with the economic is found in Stephen D. Krasner, *Defending the National Interest: Raw Materials Investments and U.S. Foreign Policy* (Princeton: Princeton University Press, 1978), pp. 31-34; G. John Ikenberry, "Conclusion: An Institutional Approach to American Foreign Economic Policy," in G. John Ikenberry, David A. Lake, and Michael Mastanduno, eds., *The State and American Foreign Economic Policy* (Ithaca, N.Y.: Cornell University Press, 1988), pp. 219-243.

2. Roy McLaren, "Road from Marrakech," *Canadian Foreign Policy* 2 (Spring 1994): 5.

3. Joseph Grunwald, "The Rocky Road Toward Hemispheric Economic Integration: A Regional Background with Attention to the Future," in Richard S. Belous and Jonathan Lemco, eds., *NAFTA as a Model of Development* (Washington, D.C.: National Planning Association, 1993), pp. 51-67.

4. Gary Clyde Hufbauer, ed., *Europe 1992: An American Perspective* (Washington, D.C.: Brookings Institution, 1990).

5. Peter Morici, *Meeting the Competitive Challenge: Canada and the United States in the Global Economy* (Washington, D.C.: National Planning Association, 1988); Frederic C. Menz and Sarah A. Stevens, *Economic Opportunities in Freer U.S. Trade with Canada* (Albany: State University of New York Press, 1991).

6. Gustavo Vega-Canovas is particularly good on this point in "Comment on Robert Pastor, 'NAFTA as Center of Integration Process,'" in Nora Lustig, Barry D. Bosworth, and Robert Z. Lawrence, eds., *North American Free Trade: Assessing the Impact* (Washington, D.C.: Brookings Institution, 1992), pp. 199-204.

7. For the capacity of Mexico to sustain greater trade openness, see Manuel Pastor and Carol Wise, "The Origins and Sustainability of Mexico's Free Trade Policy," *International Organization* 48, 3 (Summer 1994): 459-489.

8. Delal Baer, "North American Free Trade," *Foreign Affairs* 70 (Fall 1991): 132-149.

9. Sidney Weintraub, *A Marriage of Convenience: Relations Between Mexico and the United States* (New York: Oxford University Press, 1990).

10. Edward John Ray, "Changing Patterns of Protectionism: The Fall in Tariffs and the Rise in Non-tariff Barriers," in Jeffry A. Freiden and David A. Lake, eds., *International Political Economy: Perspectives on Global Power and Wealth*, 2nd ed. (New York: St. Martin's Press, 1991), pp. 338-352.

11. Charles F. Doran, "North-South Relations and Foreign Aid Reform: A Realistic Approach," Walter Sterling Surrey Memorial Lecture, Washington, D.C., 1994.

12. Arnold J. Toynbee, *A Study of History: Abridgement of Volumes I-VI*, by D. C. Somervell (New York: Oxford University Press, 1946), p. 288.

13. Ibid.

14. Peter H. Smith, *Mexico: Neighbor in Transition* Headline series no. 267 (Washington, D.C.: Foreign Policy Association, 1984).

15. James Goldsborough, "California's Foreign Policy," *Foreign Affairs* 72 (Spring 1993): 88-96.

16. Some analysts explain these countervailing trends in terms of upward and downward "identities." See Stephen Blank and Leonard Waverman, "The Changing Infrastructure of North America and Its Impact on Canada's Relations with Latin America," in Jerry Haar and Edgar J. Dosman, eds., *A Dynamic Partnership: Canada's Changing Role in the Hemisphere* (New Brunswick, N.J.: Transaction, 1993), p. 8; William Wallace, *The Transformation of Western Europe* (New York: Council on Foreign Relations, 1990).

17. In theoretical terms this problem, the tension between opposing trends of societal change, further complicates the "economic geography" model that Paul Krugman develops and exemplifies in the Canada-U.S. case. Factor flows are not just multiple, nonlinear, bidirectional, and capable of peripheralizing a nonmature economy. Core and periphery are continually under pressure to centralize and decentralize, to unify and frag-ment. This potential for "reaggregation" must also be built into the economic spacial model. Krugman, *Geography and Trade* (Louven [Louvain]: Leuven University Press; Cambridge, Mass.: MIT Press, 1991), p. 91.

18. Peter Katzenstein aptly describes Germany in terms of a "decentralized state and a centralized society." Peter J. Katzenstein, *Policy and Politics in West Germany: The Growth of the Semisovereign State* (Philadelphia: Temple University Press, 1987), pp. 15-34.

19. Earl H. Fry, "The Subnationalism Dilemma," in "Sectoral Free Trade Between Canada and the United States: A U.S. Perspective," in Lee H. Radebaugh and Earl H. Fry, eds., Canada/U.S. Trade Relations (Provo, Utah: Brigham Young University Press, 1984), p. 47.

5

Social Policy in a North American Free-Trade Area

Keith G. Banting

The North American Free Trade Agreement (NAFTA) among the United States, Canada, and Mexico adds to the growing evidence that international trade regimes are developing a social dimension. As trade agreements have lowered tariffs and constrained other traditional nontariff barriers, attention has increasingly focused on the competitive implications of different standards in social programs, labor protection, and environmental regulation. The side agreements that accompanied the adoption of the NAFTA have entrenched labor and environmental concerns in the North American trade system, and stand as a visible symbol of an emerging trend in the international trading regime.

Concern about the tension between trade liberalization and the social role of the state has progressed through two phases in recent years. The first phase was sparked by the emergence of regional trading blocs among countries of broadly comparable levels of economic development. In Europe, the Maastricht proposals for a single market prompted fears in countries such as Germany that their ambitious social programs and labor protection would place them at a competitive disadvantage, and that they would face powerful pressures to lower their standards to compete with less generous European neighbors. In response to those fears, the European Union adopted the Social Charter. Similarly, in North America, the original Free Trade Agreement (FTA) between the United States and Canada sparked an intense debate among Canadians about whether their more generous social programs could survive closer integration with the economic colossus to the south. Although the FTA did not incorporate an explicit social dimension, controversy about its impact on health care and other social programs during the 1988 Canadian election almost derailed the agreement.

NAFTA opened the second phase of the debate, in which free-trade blocs were extended to incorporate countries at much different levels of economic development and with very different social policies. The side deals that were negotiated as the price for ratification of the NAFTA placed developing nations on notice that the price of more complete access to the markets of the first world would include some protection for the social dimensions of state activity. The importance of this issue was underscored in the last moment of the Uruguay Round when the United States and France pushed for the addition of a "social dumping" clause to the General Agreement on Tariffs and Trade (GATT). Although the proposal was not adopted, it suggests that social issues will be an important element in the next round of world trade talks.

Proposals for a social dimension to trade agreements provoke strong disagreement between developed and developing nations. On one side, developed countries such as the United States and Canada fear that their more expansive social commitments will constitute a competitive disadvantage under NAFTA, leaving them with an unpalatable choice between watching more jobs flow south and dismantling their social and regulatory programs. On the other hand, developing countries such as Mexico fear that social and environmental concerns represent the new face of protectionism. They suspect that rich countries, having been deprived of their traditional means of trade discrimination, will exploit differences in social programs to achieve the same effect.

Although these issues have generated intense political and polemical debates, there has been remarkably little careful empirical research that investigates the impact of closer economic integration on the social role of the state. Is it true that deeper integration generates irresistible pressures for closer harmonization of social and regulatory regimes? What are the social implications of closer economic integration for the United States, Canada, and Mexico?

To shed some initial light on these questions, this chapter focuses on the patterns of convergence and divergence in the social policies of Canada and the United States during the 1980s and early 1990s.[1] This represents an interesting test for two reasons. First, although the

Canadian welfare state is not particularly generous by the standards of northern Europe, there is a clear contrast with the United States. In Canada, universal health and social security programs provide more comprehensive protection for the population as a whole; a stronger set of selective programs target more resources on low-income Canadians; and the system as a whole provides for a higher level of vertical redistribution. Second, the 1980s and early 1990s represented a period of change in social policy. The reality of intense global competition and the deep integration of the Canadian and American economies became clearer to both policy-makers and their electorates, and important social programs in both countries were subjected to successive waves of retrenchment and restructuring in response to the new pressures. Was the result a convergence in the design of social programs? Or did the period witness further divergence in the Canadian and American patterns of social protection?

Obviously, the experience of phase one of the North American trading bloc cannot provide definitive conclusions about the probable social consequences of its extension to Mexico under the NAFTA. Nevertheless, as we shall see, the indications are interesting, and should provide some reassurance to those who fear the worst.

The chapter is organized in three sections. The first section summarizes the debate about the relationship between economic integration and social policy that resonated in Canada during the 1980s. The second section examines social programs in Canada and the United States since the early 1980s. The final section returns to the larger questions posed by the NAFTA.

THE CONTROVERSY

During the great debates of the 1980s, Canadian critics of the FTA saw a double-barreled threat to social programs. First, they feared that Canadian social programs that raised the costs of production above those in the United States would drive jobs and investment south; Canadian business would then lobby for lower social commitments; and Canadian governments would have little choice but to comply. Second, critics feared that Canadian programs such as health care that lowered the costs of production by socializing costs borne by American employers would be interpreted in the United States as subsidies and subjected to countervail and other trade action. In either case, the result would be convergence between the two social policy regimes, with the burden of adjustment falling on Canada.

Defenders of closer continental ties during the 1980s insisted that economic integration does not necessitate policy harmonization. After all, they insisted, Canada's distinctive social programs were actually developed in a period when the Canadian and American economies were becoming more deeply entwined, and the country would continue to be free to pursue more ambitious social goals in a closer North American context. Programs financed by taxes that reduced net real incomes rather than increasing the costs of production would present no problem; and programs that increased business costs would simply trigger a compensating change in the exchange rate. Whereas individual programs that implicitly provided selective subsidies to specific industrial sectors or regions, such as development grants or the special benefits for fishermen under unemployment insurance, might be vulnerable to trade challenges, social programs that were generally available in Canada would be immune from such actions.

The next section of this chapter addresses this debate by looking for patterns of convergence and divergence in the social programs on the two sides of the border, and assesses the reasons for cases of convergence that do emerge. Convergence in the programs of two countries can, of course, emerge for a number of reasons other than the immediate economic links between them. Indeed, it is possible to conceive of four possibilities:

1. Convergence as a result of parallel domestic factors. Convergence in policy regimes can emerge because the two countries face similar problems, experience similar domestic political responses to them, or learn from each other's experience.[2] For example, if the United States had adopted Canadian-style national health insurance during its recent debate on health reform, it would have done so because of domestic political pressures to deal with problems of cost and coverage, not because of economic competition with Canada.

2. Convergence as a direct result of economic integration. Convergence can emerge for precisely the reasons cited by Canadian critics of economic integration, as the field of corporate taxation makes compellingly clear. The history of tax reform during the 1980s demonstrates a conviction within the Canadian government that imposing higher corporate taxes than the United States would risk serious erosion of its tax base and revenues.[3]

3. Convergence as an indirect result of economic integration. Convergence might also emerge more slowly, as a secondary consequence of changes induced by economic integration. For example, if closer integration seriously erodes Canadian economic performance compared with that of its regional trading partners, social programs could not escape downstream effects. Similarly, if economic integration leads to greater cultural convergence with the United States, reshaping the preferences that Canadians bring to their politics, differences in social programs would narrow over time.

4. Convergence as a result of wider global integration. Convergence between Canada and the United States could also emerge as the North American echo of wider trends. The globalization of the economy, the intensity of international trade, and the painful restructuring of traditional industries have generated common policy debates in many nations, often led by organizations such as the OECD, the World Bank, and others. For example, the growing emphasis on human capital development as the key to comparative advantage in the future has stimulated remarkably similar debates about education and training in many nations.

Separating these different dynamics in specific cases of convergence is not easy, and assessing the longer-term relationships is particularly difficult over a short time frame. Nevertheless, these distinctions are useful, as an examination of social policies of Canada and the United States suggests.

CONVERGENCE AND DIVERGENCE IN THE 1980s AND 1990s

In searching for patterns of convergence and divergence between Canada and the United States, much depends on the programs chosen for examination; for example, contemporary debates in the two countries over education and training or child care are very similar. During the 1980s, however, Canadian concerns centred primarily on health care and income security, and this section therefore concentrates on those sectors.

Health Care

Traditionally, health care has provided the most dramatic contrast between Canada and the United States, and that contrast became more marked in the 1980s and early 1990s. The basic outlines of the public health insurance programs in Canada and the United States are reasonably familiar. In Canada, Medicare provides comprehensive hospital and medical services on a universal basis; private health insurance is limited to a narrow range of supplementary benefits; and private expenditures represent only a quarter of total health spending. In the United States, public programs cover only specific categories of the population: Medicare provides health insurance for the elderly; Veterans Affairs provides fuller coverage for elderly and disabled veterans; and Medicaid, a means-tested program delivered by state governments, provides health care to about 42 percent of the nation's poor. The rest of the American population must rely on the private sector. However, private coverage is seriously incomplete: approximately 13 percent of the population—mostly low-income workers and their families—are without any coverage, and another 8 percent are seriously underinsured.[4]

The contrast between the two systems has grown sharper in recent years. The intense pressure on health-care costs has been at the heart of health-care politics in both countries, but the Canadian single-payer system has coped more successfully. In 1971, the two countries devoted similar proportions of their national resources to health expenditures, but by 1989 health expenditures represented a considerably lower share of GNP in Canada.[5] This has been accomplished without abandoning universality of access. Some provinces have introduced marginal restrictions on the range of medical services covered by public health insurance, and there has been some growth in the role of private health insurance. However, the 1984 Canada Health Act largely blocked the introduction of fees and co-payments. So far, at least, the balance between public and private sectors in health care has changed only at the margins.

In contrast, health insurance coverage in the United States has eroded since the 1980s. Despite a relentless search for new mechanisms of cost control, health expenditures continue their relentless climb, reaching 13 percent of GNP in 1991 and putting severe strain on the budgets of both governments and private employers. Employers have responded by transferring more of the burden onto employees through reduced coverage and increased deductibles and co-payments; and in many small firms, health insurance has disappeared completely. These trends have been exacerbated by the long-term shift in employment from manufacturing to services, where coverage tends to be lower, and by the recession, because unemployed workers normally lose their health benefits along with their jobs. Nor are public programs responding to the growing need. Despite recent federal initiatives to expand Medicaid eligibility for pregnant women and for children, increasingly restrictive state rules seem to be reducing the program's overall reach; and sharp limits on reimbursement rates are reducing the willingness of doctors and hospitals to accept large numbers of Medicaid patients. The cumulative effect is hardly surprising: the percentage of Americans with no health coverage at all rose by more than a third between 1979 and 1986, and the number with inadequate coverage also continues to grow.[6]

Thus the two health-care systems diverged further along traditional lines during the 1980s. Whether the late 1990s will see a continuation of this trend, or whether there will be important elements of convergence is discussed below.

Pensions

The overall role of the state in providing retirement income for the elderly is similar in Canada and the United States, with public programs providing comparable portions of the income of those aged sixty-five and over on both sides of the border. As Table 5.1 suggests, the biggest difference lies in the more redistributive character of the benefit structure in Canada. This table overstates the cross-national difference somewhat because it does not incorporate the

Table 5.1
Replacement Ratios, Canada and the United States, 1989: Public Retirement Benefits as a Proportion of Preretirement Earnings for New Retirees

	Low Earnings	Average Earnings	High Earnings
United States	57.9	41.7	24.1
Canada			
Without GIS	61.0	44.6	22.3
With GIS	86.5	50.7	22.3

Source: Ratios for Canada calculated from benefit levels reported in National Council on Welfare, *Welfare Incomes 1990*, 1991, Tables 4 and 5; ratios for the United States from U. S. House of Representatives, Committee on Ways and Means, *Overview of Entitlement Programs: 1990 Green Book*, 1990, Appendix A, Table 15.

means-tested Supplementary Security Income (SSI) in the calculations for the United States. It is difficult to include a means-tested benefit in replacement ratios because assets as well as income constitute a major consideration in determining eligibility. Nevertheless, the general impression conveyed by Table 5.1 is undoubtedly correct. SSI reaches such a tiny portion of the elderly (only 6.6 percent in 1988) that most low-income retired people do not receive it. In contrast, nearly half of the entire elderly population in Canada, including many with average earnings before retirement, received a Guaranteed Income Supplement (GIS) payment during the mid-1980s.

The politics of the 1980s and 1990s have accentuated this difference. Frontal assaults on major benefits were repulsed on both sides of the border, and only more limited adjustments survived the political process. Nevertheless, the burden of the changes fell differently in the two countries. Changes in U.S. legislation spread the pain evenly, with rich and poor recipients bearing the same proportionate reduction in their replacement rates.[7] In Canada, however, the redistributive impact of the system was increased by a significant enrichment of the GIS in the early 1980s and the claw-back of Old Age Security (OAS) from high-income recipients at the end of the decade. As Coder, Smeeding, and Torrey demonstrated in a study of poverty among the elderly in Canada, the United States, and Australia, changes in transfer programs between 1981 and 1987 reduced the number of Canadian elderly living in poverty much more than in the United States: in terms of winner and losers, the 1980s "saw the low-income elderly in Canada as big winners."[8] Once again, traditional differences have been increasing, not shrinking.

Unemployment Insurance

In the early 1990s, Canadian critics of the U.S.-Canada Free Trade Agreement (FTA) argued that unemployment insurance provided evidence of the corrosive effects of the FTA.

Since 1971, the Canadian program has provided greater protection to the unemployed than its American counterpart, and has represented a much larger financial commitment for the public sector. For example, in 1987 government expenditures for unemployment benefits represented 3.2 percent of GDP in Canada, but only 0.4 percent in the United States.[9] This difference in the size of the two programs grew

Figure 5.1
Unemployment Insurance Recipients as a Proportion of Unemployed Workers: Canada and the United States, 1968-1993

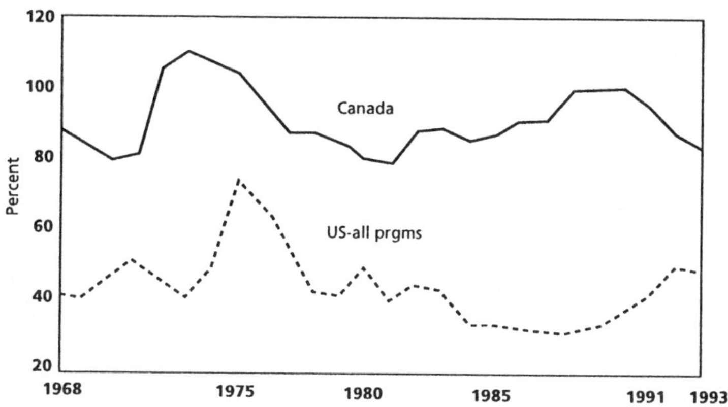

Source: Calculated from data in U. S. House of Representatives, Committee on Ways and Means, *Overview of Entitlement Programs: 1994 Green Book*, 1994, and Statistics Canada, *Canadian Economic Observer: Historical Statistical Supplement 1993/94*, 1994.

strongly over the course of the 1980s, as Figure 5.1 demonstrates. Although the Canadian program had undergone retrenchment in the late 1970s, it suffered only marginal adjustments during the more traumatic decade of the 1980s. The Reagan administration, however, had a dramatic impact on unemployment insurance south of the border. Federal legislation virtually eliminated a system of extended benefits, which had previously been triggered during recessions, and began to charge interest on state borrowing from the federal Treasury, which put pressure on states to revise their programs. Given the weakness of organized labor in most state capitals, the revisions relied much more on reduced benefits than increased payroll taxes. According to Burtless, the result was a serious erosion of unemployment insurance that went "virtually unnoticed in the early 1980s at a time when far smaller proportional cutbacks in public assistance, disability insurance and social security caused loud public outcries."[10]

Divergence in the 1980s has given way to an element of convergence in the 1990s. Retrenchment in the Canadian program in 1991 was attacked by many critics as a clear example of harmonization with the American model in the aftermath of the Free Trade Agreement, and further changes in 1994 have intensified the concern. Certainly the changes have reduced the difference in qualification periods, benefit duration, and benefit levels between the median state program in the United States and the Canadian program in affluent (i.e., high employment) regions. In addition, the United States has temporarily repaired some of the damage to its program. After protracted political battles between president and Congress, benefits for victims of the recession were extended in late 1991 and again in early 1992.

Nevertheless, it is important not to overstate the convergence here. As Figure 5.1 suggests, until the end of 1993 the changes had not fully offset the large differences between the programs.[11]

Child Benefits

Child benefits are the sector in which we are seeing the strongest convergence. In the mid-1970s, the contrast between the two countries was clear. Canada had a universal system of family allowances, as well as a tax exemption for dependent children. The United States was as the only major industrialized nation with no general child allowance program other than tax exemptions for dependent children.

Since then, the contrast has faded as both countries have experimented with the integration of the tax and transfer systems in order to provide more targeted support for low-income families. In the early 1970s, the United States introduced a refundable earned income tax credit (EITC) for working-poor families with children. Although the EITC has been enriched a number of times since then, it still has limited reach. As a credit against earned income, it provides no support for welfare families who have no earnings, and its benefits are low for larger families.[12]

Canada has moved even more strongly in the same direction. In 1978, the federal government introduced the refundable child tax credit (RCTC), financed in part by a reduction in the universal family allowances. From the outset, the RCTC was a broader benefit than the EITC, providing support to both the working poor and the welfare poor, and directing higher payments to larger families. In the years after 1978, a complicated set of changes moved the system further toward this model. The trend has culminated in a new child benefits program, which replaces the universal system of family allowances completely and establishes a single, income-tested payment for children.

Child benefits in the two countries have clearly converged since the early 1980s. The traditional contrast generated by the Canadian system of universal family allowances has given way to variations on a common theme of income-tested benefits operating in parallel with or through the tax system.

Public Assistance

The pattern of divergence rather than convergence reasserts itself when attention shifts to public assistance. Canada has a tradition of stronger redistribution to the poor through this instrument. Under the terms of the Canada Assistance Plan, provinces must provide assistance to all persons in need. The level of support provided to different family types does vary, and the support provided to single individuals is quite limited in some provinces. Nevertheless, support is to be provided to everyone in need. Coverage in the United States is less complete. Traditionally, aid to families with dependent children (AFDC) was restricted to single-parent families, but by the late 1980s about half of the states extended support to the children in two-parent households when the principal wage earner was unemployed. Since 1990, states have been required to provide this broader coverage, but only for six months in any year. Moreover, single persons and childless couples remain ineligible. Income support for these people is limited to food stamps, a federal program, and general assistance, a purely state and/or local program which provides meager benefits and does not exist at all in almost half of the states. In addition to differences in coverage, benefit levels have traditionally been higher in Canada. For example, Blank and Hanratty found that in 1986, "even in the least-generous province in Canada, the SA (social assistance) benefit level for single-parent families exceeds the maximum low-income transfer (AFDC and Food Stamps) available in all states except Alaska."[13]

Table 5.2
U. S. Public Assistance Benefits, 1975-1990 (1985 constant dollars)

Benefit	1975	1980	1985	1990	% Change 75/90
Maximum AFDC monthly payment					
3-person family	462	388	326	315	-31.8
4-person family	542	449	389	372	-31.4
Maximum combined AFDC/Food Stamp monthly payment					
3-person family	670	576	526	511	-23.7
4-person family	812	694	647	613	-24.5

Source: Compiled by the author from data in P. Peterson and M. Rom, *Welfare Magnets: A New Case for a National Standard* (Washington, D.C.: Brookings Institution, 1990), Table 1-1.

These differentials grew strongly into the early 1990s. In the United States, AFDC payments have undergone a long-term decline that has been only partially cushioned by food stamps, as Table 5.2 indicates. This trend reflects the failure to index benefits fully for inflation since the mid-1970s, as well as explicit cutbacks in both eligibility and benefits during the last years of the Carter presidency and the early years of the Reagan administration. The 1988 Family Support Act did seek to increase training opportunities for welfare recipients, and the legislation did introduce the requirement (mentioned earlier) that as of 1990, states must assist needy two-parent families for at least half the year. Nevertheless, the pattern of decline in real terms accelerated in the early 1990s. State governments face a fiscal crisis familiar to that of Canadian provinces: depressed revenues and increased welfare costs; intense pressure on expenditures for health care; new federal mandates but reduced federal grants; and public resistance to tax increases. Unlike their Canadian counterparts, however, state budgetmakers cannot increase their deficits. Forty-nine states are required by their constitutions or state

Table 5.3
Change in Public Assistance Benefits, Canada and the United States, 1985-1992 (in percentages)

Beneficiaries	Province or State Average	Weighted Average
Canada[a]		
Single Parent, one child	+3.3	+10.7
Couple, two children	+3.8	+11.6
United States[b]		
Mother, two children	-2.4	- 2.9

[a]Data for Canada represent 1986-1992.
[b]U.S. benefits include both AFDC and Food Stamps.

Source: Data on benefits from National Council on Welfare, *Welfare Incomes 1994* (Ottawa: The Council, 1994), Table 5; U.S. House of Representatives, Committee on Ways and Means, *Overview of Entitlement Programs: 1993 Green Book* (1993), pp. 1251-1253.

law to balance their budgets. The result in 1991 was a wave of reductions in AFDC and, especially, general assistance. Cuts were most dramatic in Michigan—which abolished general assistance altogether—and in Massachusetts, but also significant in states as diverse as California, Maryland, Ohio, Illinois, Maine, and the District of Columbia. Many other states simply froze benefit levels.[14]

Although comparable long-term data are unavailable in Canada, benefits did not decline in the same way. During the early 1980s the three westernmost provinces did reduce welfare rates, but most other provinces maintained their benefits in real terms.[15] The record of the second half of the decade was equally mixed. Although benefits in several provinces did decline marginally in real terms between 1986 and 1990, other provinces maintained or enriched the real value of their benefits, with particularly strong increases in Ontario and Quebec.[16] Table 5.3 demonstrates the direction of change in the two countries during the years for which comparable data exist. This divergence may not continue, as fiscal pressures build on Canadian provinces. Nevertheless, it still matters whether a poor person lives in Toronto or Detroit.

Poverty, Inequality and Redistribution

Given these trends, it is hardly surprising that the differences in the redistributive role of the state grew during the 1980s. Table 5.4 illustrates this pattern for child poverty. The redistributive gap grew in part because of a strengthening of the Canadian system, but primarily because of the weakening of the redistributive impulse in the United States. Other studies confirm the pattern for other groups. The study noted earlier on the position of the elderly in the two countries came to similar conclusions.[17] And a careful analysis of support for the nonelderly poor in Canada and the United States by Blank and Hanratty concluded that "the Canadian transfer system is substantially more effective than the U.S. transfer system in raising people out of poverty," and that the effect has become more marked with time.[18]

Trends in the distribution of income more generally follow a similar pattern. South of the border, the weakened redistributive role of government could not compensate for the growing inequality in

Table 5.4
Effect of Taxes and Transfers on Levels of Child Poverty[a] in Canada and the United States in the 1980s (percentage poor)

	Canada		United States	
	1981	1987	1979	1986
Pretax and Transfer	15.5	15.7	19.0	22.3
Postax and Transfer	10.2	09.3	14.7	20.4
Reduction	05.3	06.4	04.3	01.9
Percent Reduction	34.2	40.8	24.2	08.5

[a]Poverty is defined as 40 percent of median disposable income in each country.

Source: T. M. Smeeding, "Cross National Perspectives on Trends in Child Poverty and the Effectiveness of Government Policies in Preventing Poverty among Families with Children in the 1980s: The First Evidence from LIS," unpublished manuscript.

market incomes of the decade.[19] In Canada, however, greater inequality in market incomes was largely offset by the tax-transfer system, producing a relatively stable distribution of final income during the 1980s.[20]

THE LIMITS OF CONVERGENCE

During the 1980s and early 1990s, the broadest pattern was one of increased divergence, with traditional differences between the two countries growing in health care, pensions, public assistance, and the redistributive impact of the state. In part, this pattern has resulted from program changes in Canada; but in the main, divergence has flowed from a stronger erosion of coverage and benefits in the United States during the Reagan-Bush years.

Convergence was limited to two of the programs examined in this chapter: child benefits and unemployment insurance, with child benefits representing the more dramatic case. As noted earlier, a number of factors can underlie such convergence; and it is clear that convergence in these two programs did not flow unambiguously from closer integration of the Canadian and American economies. First, in both cases the narrowing of the gap stemmed to a significant degree from American decisions, and not even the most optimistic Canadian would attribute such changes to pressures inherent in the relationship between the two countries. Second, changes on the Canadian side were not driven exclusively by bilateral economic integration, as a closer look at child benefits and unemployment insurance suggests.

Convergence in child benefits has predominantly been a reflection of parallel domestic trends. The remaking of this sector has been a slow process of incremental change rooted initially in a common ideological debate about the nature of poverty and the interaction between tax and transfer systems, a debate that first emerged during the 1960s and 1970s in the form of proposals for a negative income tax. From the beginning, reform efforts on both sides of the border were also fueled by economic issues, especially concerns about the perverse incentives facing those dependent on traditional welfare programs; and in more recent years these concerns have been reinforced by the impact of globalization and international trade on the prospects for low-skilled and displaced workers in developed nations generally. Nevertheless, common ideological trends rather than economic integration between Canada and the United States seem to be the predominant factor in the convergence in child benefits. It could be argued that this pattern reflects a broader cultural integration of the two countries that flows with a lag from closer economic links, but such an argument would have to contend with the interest in similar ideas in Britain and other nations during the same period.[21]

Unemployment insurance is more contentious. As noted earlier, the changes in 1991 and 1994 in Canada and the 1991-92 changes in the United States have narrowed the differences in qualification and benefit provisions, although, as Figure 5.1 indicated, the convergence is far from complete. Concern for economic competition between the two countries may have been part of the calculus in Canada, but it was certainly not all-pervasive in shaping recent changes. A special benefit for fishermen, which has been a source of trade friction with the United States, was retained; regional differentials in benefits, which some analysts suggest will be undermined by economic integration with the United States, have remained entrenched in the program; changes in the financing of the program in the 1980s increased rather than decreased employer costs; and the new administrative structure for the program points to corporatist traditions absent in the United States.

It seems more plausible to interpret the changes on the Canadian side as the product of domestic conservatism, fiscal constraint, and the pressures on labor markets and educational policy more generally. These pressures clearly go beyond the provisions of the Free Trade Agreement and the economic relationship with the United States more narrowly defined. They parallel a debate about the balance between income support and training programs that pervades OECD nations.

In general, this survey offers limited support for the proposition that closer economic integration of Canada and the United States necessitates social policy convergence. The record of the 1980s and 1990s includes divergence in many sectors, and it is arguable that the Canadian and American welfare states are as different today as they were in the late 1970s. Moreover, where convergence has taken place, it is difficult to establish a simple link to economic integration between the two countries.

There is, of course, one major qualification to this conclusion. The full effects of closer North American integration have yet to reveal themselves. As those effects work their way through the system during the 1990s, we may witness more dramatic examples of convergence. This is particularly important in the case of the longer-term, indirect effects of economic integration. If the closer continental embrace erodes Canadian economic performance relative to that of the United States, if the net effect of the FTA in the longer term is to undermine productivity growth and employment north of the border, then the fiscal base of Canadian governments will decline further and the squeeze on social programs will intensify.

Even if Canadian economic performance does not erode compared with that of the United States, the proposition that the 1990s will see more examples of convergence is plausible. Fiscal pressures on governments are already stronger north of the border, and some of the divergence of the 1980s and early 1990s may fade in years to come. As noted earlier, several provinces have already deinsured a small number of medical procedures, and this process of narrowing the range of services deemed essential will undoubtedly continue as federal transfers to the provinces decline. Benefits for the unemployed and for social assistance recipients remain politically vulnerable. However, changes are most likely to accentuate the trend that has been developing since the mid-1960s, with a larger portion of income-security expenditures flowing through targeted as opposed to universal programs, a pattern that diverges from the American trend.

Overall, however, the past is likely to be a reasonable guide to the future. The late 1990s are apt to see areas of convergence and areas of divergence in the social policy structures of Canada and the United States.

NAFTA AND THE FUTURE

What conclusions can be drawn from Canadian and American social policies under the FTA for future relations among the three economic partners that have been joined by NAFTA? Obviously, such an exercise must be approached with caution. The much greater economic and social differences among the partners, and the addition of side agreements on labor and the environment represent differences of character rather than of degree. Nevertheless, several observations seem relevant.

The first is a warning to avoid determinist interpretations. Predictions that economic integration necessitates policy harmonization, whether in the context of the single European market or of North American free trade, assume that future policy decisions will be shaped more by international economics than by domestic politics. Although international pressures on the state have clearly grown, the demise of the nation-state as an independent force has been greatly overstated. Each nation must adjust to powerful international economic pressures, but economic forces do not dictate the way in which each country responds. Policy is also shaped by domestic politics, and different countries will respond to the changing world differently.

The second observation concerns the cyclical role of issues in trade policy. It is striking that social policy played a much more limited role in Canadian debates over the ratification of the NAFTA than during the debate over the FTA. In part, the change reflected the different dynamic implicit in Mexico's accession to the bloc. The FTA joined two countries with broadly comparable economies, wage structures, and productivity levels; in that context, differences in social programs were seen as potentially important. In the case of NAFTA and Mexico, the dramatic differentials in wages and their implications for the location of manufacturing activity dominated debate in Canada, with the linkage between economic integration and social policy being seen as much more indirect. However, the secondary role played by social policy in the Canadian debate over the NAFTA was also the result of experience during the FTA period. The reality was that the 1980s and early 1990s provided little evidence of substantial convergence in the social programs of Canada and the United States, or of trade disputes emerging from differences in social policies. This suggests that the politics of trade policy is, in part, a learning process, and that issues wax and wane as experience confirms or challenges predictions that dominated the previous trading round.

One must be careful, however, about automatically assuming that the NAFTA experience will parallel that of the FTA, and that concern over labor and environmental issues will fade with experience. Unlike the FTA, the NAFTA actually entrenches environmental and labor issues in the trade regime through side agreements and the formal machinery set out in them. These structures will undoubtedly legitimate and stimulate trade-related conflict over environmental and labor issues. This is especially true of environmental concerns. Unlike the labour accord, the environmental deal calls for the creation of a Joint Public Advisory Committee, which has the potential to become a forum for promoting environmental concerns on a NAFTA-wide basis, and explicitly allows third parties to initiate formal complaints against one of the countries through the environmental secretariat. Admittedly, the complex dispute resolution mechanisms set out in both agreements were designed to minimize the extent to which trade sanctions or fines actually result. Nevertheless, Canadian experience with the FTA suggests that private interests in the United States will seek to employ fully all of the possibilities inherent in the formal agreements.[22]

We can therefore expect that social issues will pervade trade relations under NAFTA more completely than under the FTA. Nevertheless, the experience of the FTA and social policy continues to stand as a reminder of the tenacity of national differences in social affairs. The social role carved out by the state reflects important features of the culture and political interests of the society of which it is part. Although the globalization of economic life and the trading agreements that give it life obviously constrain what modern governments can do, the politics within the nation-state retains its social importance.

NOTES

1. The research on which this chapter is based was generously funded by the Donner Canadian Foundation as part of the project Canada and the United States in a Changing Global Context. An earlier version of part of this chapter was published as "Integracion economica y convergencia social: La politica social canadiense en una economia norteamericana," in Gustavo Vega Canovas, ed., *Mexico Estados Unidos Canada 1991-1992* (Mexico City: Colegio de Mexico, 1993).

2. For a symposium on the processes through which nations learn from the policy experience of other countries, see *Journal of Public Policy*, 11, no. 1 (1991).

3. W. Alpert, J. Shoven, and J. Whalley, "Introduction," in J. Shoven and J. Whalley, *Canada-U.S. Tax Comparisons* (Chicago: University of Chicago Press, 1992).

4. See chapter 1 of U.S. Bipartisan Commission on Comprehensive Health

Care, the Pepper Commission, *A Call to Action: Final Report* (Washington, D.C.: Government Printing Office, 1990).

5. See U.S. General Accounting Office, *Canadian Health Insurance: Lessons for the United States* (Washington, D.C.: U.S. General Accounting Office, 1991).

6. United States Bipartisan Commission on Comprehensive Health Care, 1990, chapter 1.

7. See U. S. House of Representatives, Committee on Ways and Means, *Overview of Entitlement Programs: 1994 Green Book* (Washington, D.C.: Government Printing Office, 1994), Table I-7.

8. J. Coder, T. Smeeding and B. Torrey, "The Change in the Economic Status of the Low-Income Elderly in Three Industrial Countries: Circa 1977-1986," paper for the Bureau of the Census' 1990 Annual Research Conference, Washington, D.C., 1990.

9. OECD, *OECD in Figures: Statistics on the Member Countries, 1989 Edition*. Supplement to *The OECD Observer*, no. 158 (Paris: OECD, 1989).

10. G. Burtless, "The Tattered Saftey Net," *Brookings Review*, 9 (1991): 38-41. See also L. Hansen and J. Beyers, eds., *Unemployment Insurance: The Second Half-Century* (Madison: University of Wisconsin Press, 1990).

11. In Figure 5.1, the Canadian ratio can rise above 100 because some recipients are recorded as discouraged workers and not counted as unemployed by the Labour Force Survey. In the United States, "all programs" includes both regular state benefits and supplementary and extended benefits.

12. U.S. House of Representatives, Committee on Ways and Means, *Overview of Entitlement Programs: 1991 Green Book*, (Washington, D.C.: Government Printing Office, 1991), p. 897.

13. R. Blank and M. Hanratty, "Responding to Need: A Comparison of Social Safety Nets in the United States and Canada," in D. Card and R. Freeman, eds., *Small Differences that Matter: Labor Markets and Income Maintenance in Canada and the United States* (Chicago: Chicago University Press, 1993), p. 197.

14. Center on Budget and Policy Priorities and Center for the Study of the States, *The States and the Poor: How Budget Decisions in 1991 Affected Low Income People* (Washington, D.C., 1991).

15. K. G. Banting, "The Welfare State and Inequality in the 1980s," *Canadian Review of Sociology and Anthropology*, 24 (1987): 309-338.

16. National Council of Welfare, *Welfare Incomes 1990* (Ottawa: The Council, 1991).

17. Coder, Smeeding, and Torrey, "The Change in the Economic Status of the Low-Income Elderly," 1990.

18. Blank and Hanratty, "Responding to Need," 1993.

19. U.S. House of Representatives, Committee on Ways and Means,

Overview of Entitlement Programs: 1991 Green Book (Washington, D.C. Government Printing Office, 1991): 1183-1262.

20. J. Davies, "Tax Incidence: Annual and Lifetime Perspectives in the United States and Canada," in J. Shoven and J. Whalley, eds., *Canada-U.S. Tax Comparisons*, 1992; K. G. Banting, "Economic Integration and Policy Harmonization: Convergence and Divergence in Social Policy in Canada and the United States," in T. Hunsley, ed., *Social Policy in the Global Economy* (Kingston, Ontario: School of Policy Studies, Queens University, 1992).

21. K. G. Banting, *Poverty, Politics and Policy: Britain in the 1960s* (London: Macmillan, 1979); L. Lenkowsky, *Politics, Economics and Welfare Reform: The Failure of the Negative Income Tax in Britain and the United States* (Lanham, MD: University Press of America, 1986).

22. It was the experience of the FTA that made Canada especially opposed to the inclusion of trade sanctions which could be used by domestic American interests to harass Canadian exporters. In the end, both side deals exempted Canada completely from the possibility of trade sanctions being imposed. For a Canadian assessment of the NAFTA, see C. B. Cadsby and K. Woodside, "The Effects of the North American Free Trade Agreement on the Canada-United States Trade Relationship," *Canadian Public Policy*, 9, no. 4 (1993): 450-462.

6

Emerging Cooperation: Case of the NAFTA Commissions

Rafael Fernandez de Castro and Claudia Ibarguen

Since 1990 the United States and Mexico have undergone a period of unprecedented cooperation. In the past, this relationship had experienced few moments of collaboration, and had instead been focused on the "differences" and "antagonisms" which had been constant throughout the history of the two nations. The path traversed by the two countries in their mutual dealings had been tortuous. When the relationship did not deteriorate to total indifference, conflict was more the norm than the exception. Moreover, each country usually turned its attention to the other only during periods of friction, and with a skeptical attitude.

During the century from Mexican independence in 1821 until the 1920s, the U.S. and Mexican governments experienced a relationship in which conflict was the rule. The cold war inaugurated an era in which the principal characteristic of U.S. policy toward Mexico was negligence. The 1990s, however, represent a different period, one in which the attitudes of the two governments towards each other have drastically shifted from conflict or indifference to cooperation. This chapter will explore this intergovernmental cooperation in two emerging issue areas: labor and environment. It will be argued that the bilateral relationship between Mexico and the United States will develop lasting and continuing cooperative ties. In particular, the creation of the environmental and labor commissions by the parallel accords will foster cooperation by augmenting the quantity and quality of information, and by establishing clear rules and normative patterns that guide behavior of the actors involved in U.S.-Mexican environmental and labor affairs.

THE DAWNING OF A NEW ERA

It is evident that the bilateral relation has been transformed dramatically. Both global and national developments facilitated this shift. At the systemic level, the world scenario changed dramatically with the end of the cold war. According to a high level U.S. State Department official, the closer relation with Mexico represented the beginning of a post-cold war cooperative framework.[1] At the state level, within Mexico the emergence of a new bilateral partnership can be attributed to the dramatic transformation of the Mexican economy, which liberalized in a very short period.[2] This liberalization laid the groundwork for an impressive increase in bilateral economic arrangements.[3] Another important development that occurred within the Mexican government was the emergence of a new governing elite, the so-called technocrats. These young economists, trained in Ivy League universities, brought to the policymaking centers a renewed and positive attitude towards the United States.[4]

In the United States at least two developments can help explain the emergence of Mexican affairs as a priority in Washington's foreign policy agenda. First, the relative decline of the U.S. economy vis-à-vis the emergence of the European Community and Japan encouraged U.S. policy-makers to seek the development of a North American free-trade region. Second, a new group of Texas politicians—George Bush, James Baker, and Robert Moshbacher—took hold of the most powerful positions in Washington. Their common origin predisposed them to search for a closer, more positive association with Mexico.[5]

Once the decision was made to strengthen bilateral ties, the two governments developed new patterns for conducting U.S.-Mexican affairs. Evidence of this new and improved pattern of intergovernmental affairs can be found in almost every issue area of the bilateral relationship. The linkages between governmental agencies of the two countries grew closer and more direct. The range of federal officials involved in the relationship extended to all levels of the bureaucratic hierarchy. Twenty nine bilateral agreements were signed from 1989 to 1993, whereas only six such agreements had been concluded between 1982 and 1988. In this chapter we argue that these new ways of conducting intergovernmental affairs became a factor which reinforced and gave an element of continuity to the ongoing binational cooperation. Particular emphasis is placed on the institutionalization process in the environment and labor areas, assessing the weight that this process will have on the future of bilateral cooperation.

The North American Free Trade Agreement (NAFTA) constitutes a key element in this new U.S.-Mexican relationship. It should not be assumed, however, that NAFTA was the sole origin of cooperation. A cooperative binational framework had already begun to be established; NAFTA came to reinforce and further expand it in many areas. In some instances, such as environment and labor, NAFTA was the catalyst of closer bilateral ties.[6] NAFTA forced Mexico onto the labor and environmental policy agendas of the United States. The negotiation of NAFTA prompted labor and environmental non-governmental organizations (NGOs) in the United States, and eventually in Mexico, to participate actively in the NAFTA negotiating process. During the early stages of the negotiation, when President George Bush was seeking the reauthorization of fast track, labor unions and environmental NGOs became the most active enemies of the accord. Paradoxically, it was precisely this opposition that prompted the development of the most elaborate institutional arrangements: The North American Agreement on Labor Cooperation (NAALC) and the North American Agreement on Environmental Cooperation (NAAEC).[7]

The parallel agreements, as institutional developments, constitute the focus of this chapter. The burgeoning cooperation between the United States and Mexico will be analyzed through the prism of the institutionalization process. The objective of the analysis is to elucidate the impact of these institutional developments on the levels of cooperation in the environmental and labor areas.

THEORETICAL CONSIDERATIONS OF INSTITUTIONS AND INSTITUTION CREATION

To analyze the emerging cooperation, and particularly, to study the process of bilateral institution creation, this chapter will rely on the neoliberal institutionalist approach, a school of thought developed from the interdependence paradigm.

The bilateral relation between Mexico and the United States has been reviewed and analyzed through many lenses and perspectives.

Cooperation, however, had seldom captured the attention of scholars. This can be explained mainly by the lack of lasting and formalized government to government collaboration. In the 1980s, when the interdependence paradigm became a popular instrument for analyzing U.S.-Mexican relations, various authors began to explore bilateral cooperation. They focused, however, mainly on nongovernmental actors.[8] These scholars correctly pointed out that an inextricable link exists between the two countries. Indeed, very few neighboring nations in the world experience such an intense relationship, and the economic disparity between the two countries, makes the U.S.-Mexican relationship a unique one.

For neoliberal institutionalism to be pertinent, mutual interests must be present among the nations. This premise reduces the relevance of the theory to the market economies which share common interests. However, Robert Keohane points out that these arguments can sometimes apply to relations among developed and less-developed countries when these states have common interests which can be realized only through cooperation.[9] The relation between the United States and Mexico clearly falls under this exception. Even though the relationship is asymmetrical,[10] it is evident that the areas of interplay and commonality of interest are broad.

Keohane defines international institutions as "persistent and connected sets of rules (formal and informal) that prescribe behavioral roles, constrain activity and shape expectations"[11] Furthermore, he states, variations in the institutionalization (formalization) of world politics exert significant impacts on the behavior of governments. In particular, patterns of cooperation and discord can be understood only in the context of these international institutions. According to the degree of formalization, three different levels of institutional arrangements can be found: (1) formal intergovernmental or cross-national governmental organizations, (2) international regimes, and (3) conventions.

Formal intergovernmental or cross-national organizations are bureaucratic structures with specific rules and well-defined roles for their members. International regimes are particular sets of rules and norms that prescribe behavior in a particular issue area of international relations. Conventions are the less formalized institutions, consisting of an implicit set of rules and norms which shape the behavior of international actors.[12]

According to this theory, the U.S. and Mexican government actions and behavior will be altered by the development of bilateral institutional arrangements. It is expected that the environmental and labor parallel agreements will affect key variables in U.S.-Mexican intergovernmental affairs. As stated by Keohane, these arrangements will particularly affect the following:

—The flow of information and opportunities to negotiate
—The ability of governments to monitor each others' compliance and to implement their own commitments
—Prevailing expectations about the solidity of international agreements.[13]

The main function of the environmental and labor institutional arrangements would thus be to reduce uncertainty by establishing a stable structure of interaction between U.S. and Mexican officials.[14] By developing rules, principles and norms, these institutions establish guidelines of behavior and interaction, which can be expected to increase the possibilities of bilateral cooperation, while at the same time reducing the risk of conflict. The creation of the North American environmental and labor commissions will foster cooperation by improving the quantity and quality of information and by establishing clear rules and normative patterns to guide the behavior of actors involved in U.S.-Mexican environmental and labor affairs.

THE ENVIRONMENTAL AND LABOR CONCERNS

From the moment the U.S. and Mexican administrations decided to proceed with a free trade agreement, the prospect of entering into a free-trade agreement with a developing nation, such as Mexico, produced intense criticism in the United States. These criticisms came especially from groups that were apprehensive about job relocations and environmental degradation. Both of these concerns became focal points in the anti-NAFTA assault.

The environmental attack came mainly from environmental NGOs which feared an influx of U.S. companies to the south attracted by lax environmental enforcement in Mexico. They argued that the inability of Mexican authorities to enforce their environmental laws and regulations would prompt a massive relocation of industrial activity that would cause further damage to the border region.[15] The moderate environmental groups presented four main demands in exchange for their support of NAFTA. First, the trade agreement must not weaken or lower U.S. standards and must not prevent these standards from being raised in the future. Second, Mexico must not become a pollution haven by luring U.S. firms and jobs away through regulatory inaction. Third, U.S. firms investing in Mexico must comply with Mexican pollution control laws and compensate Mexico to allow for enforcement. Fourth, there must be some kind of sanctions to ensure environmental protection.[16]

The labor movement was more inflexible than the environmental NGOs regarding possible support of NAFTA. Trade unions raised the question of the disparity of wages and worker productivity. The U.S. unions cited widespread labor abuses in Mexico despite adequate Mexican legislation. They pointed out that Mexican resources for enforcement were scarce, so that workplace inspections were infrequent, particularly in the *maquiladora* industry, and only in rare cases were sanctions applied by inspectors. These opponents of NAFTA also maintained that disparities in working conditions between the two countries would provide Mexico with unfair trade advantages.

The labor movement thus expressed fear that (1) inadequate Mexican enforcement of labor standards,[17] and (2) the wage disparities among the two countries, would result in the erosion of U.S. labor standards and a flight of investments and jobs to Mexico to capitalize on the lower standards.[18] Both rationales centered on the main fear harbored by the U.S. labor unions, namely, the possible loss of U.S. jobs to Mexico. The principal effect of NAFTA, the AFL-CIO countered, would be to encourage the relocation of U.S. industries to Mexico. "Thousands of American workers have lost their employment, or see how their job opportunities disappear when U.S. companies relocate to take advantage of the poverty of Mexican workers and the lack of regulation on the operation of these companies."[19] The issue of jobs became, indeed, the touchstone of the NAFTA debate. The New York Times described potential job losses to Mexico as "the most potent political obstacle to Congressional approval of NAFTA."[20]

The AFL-CIO and some environmental NGO's coalesced when faced with the risk of unfair Mexican competition: enterprises escaping tough pollution standards and paying their workers a fraction of the U.S. minimum wage.[21] These two groups resembled a solid coalition during the reauthorization of fast track in the spring of 1991.[22] The coalition eventually disappeared as many "green" groups adopted NAFTA as a bargaining chip to attain some of their environmental demands.[23] The initial showdown by the environmental groups against the agreement was so effective that the Bush administration proposed a joint U.S.-Mexican environmental commission (NACE).[24] This commission's mandate, however, was limited to issuing only general assessments on environmental conditions. For the U.S. and Mexican governments, the commission represented nothing more than a forum for airing cross-border environmental disputes.[25]

From the moment Bill Clinton addressed NAFTA during his presidential campaign, he assured union leaders and environmental groups that his support for NAFTA would be conditional to the negotiation of strict parallel accords on environment and labor.[26] Early in 1993, the Clinton Administration became aware that enforcement was the key element which needed to be included into the accords. Therefore, it exerted pressure to create environmental and labor commissions with enforcement powers.

The creation of the NAALC and the NAAEC introduced further debate on the issue of institution formation to deal with a North American free-trade region. Some analysts considered that the commissions would not be sufficient to administer the ever-growing integration. Others argued that the least number of institutions should be created and that market forces should perform the necessary regulation. The mainstream environmental groups embraced NAFTA after the presentation of the NAAEC, contending that it had satisfied their minimum requirements.[27] The U.S. labor movement, despite the negotiation of new parallel accords, did not budge in their opposition to NAFTA.

ON THE PATH TO BILATERAL ENVIRONMENTAL COOPERATION

Throughout the history of U.S.-Mexican relations, environmental border problems have been present. Many of these problems can be traced to the economic disparity between the two nations, adverse climatological conditions, and the recent boom of the *maquiladora* industry. At the end of the nineteenth century, it became evident that joint efforts were necessary to face border and environmental problems. The International Boundary Commission, later the International Boundary and Water Commission (IBWC), which hails back to that period, was the first attempt to resolve, through a common organization, the problems produced by changing boundaries and a lack of water.[28]

The La Paz Agreements of 1983 were the first formalized and comprehensive environmental agreement between Mexico and the United States. Their goal was to establish areas and programs for binational cooperation. The areas were: protection, improvement, and conservation of the environment as well as prevention of emergency situations. The programs revolved basically around Article 6, which established the coordination of national programs, scientific and educational exchanges, environmental monitoring, environmental impact assessment, and periodic exchanges of information and data on likely sources of pollution in the respective territories.

The La Paz Agreements also established a mechanism for future accords and created annexes and technical assistance projects. It proposed periodic meetings of technical working groups from both countries, and high level meetings with the participation of the agreement coordinators.[29] Although the La Paz Agreements paved the way for a cooperative working relationship between the U.S. and Mexican environmental agencies, they had a number of shortfalls. Vaguely worded, many of its provisions could not be enforced, and above all, the pacts did not address the lack of financial resources in Mexico.

The reauthorization of fast track hastened a promise from President Bush that a binational border management plan would be created. In February 1992, the two governments released the Integrated Border Environmental Plan. This pact was much more comprehensive than the La Paz Agreements, addressing a wider variety of environmental issues not included in the earlier agreement.[30] The Integrated Border Environmental Plan was designed to be in effect for two years, after which it would be revised and implemented for a second phase.

The North American Agreement on Environmental Cooperation further advances the previous binational accords. It aims to promote sustainable development, cooperation on conservation, protection, and enhancement of the environment, and the effective enforcement of compliance with domestic environmental laws. The Agreement thus created a Commission for Environmental Cooperation that will oversee the achievement of its general objectives.

The most important obligation for the subscribers of the NAAEC is that they effectively enforce their own environmental laws. This commitment is backed up by a dispute settlement process, the "teeth"[31] which the environmental groups lobbied so actively to secure.

The Commission is comprised of a Council, a central Secretariat, and a Joint Public Advisory Committee. The Council, composed of the environmental ministers of each country, is the governing body of the Commission. It oversees the implementation of the Agreement, serves as the forum for discussion of environmental matters, promotes and facilitates cooperation, oversees the Secretariat, and addresses questions and disputes that may arise regarding the interpretation or application of the Agreement. The Council will be responsible for developing recommendations on public access to information. In brief, the Council has the obligation to coordinate all the activities that comprise the formulation and interchange of information among the three countries.

The Secretariat is the body created by the Commission responsible for providing technical, administrative, and operational support to the Council and to any groups established by the Council.[32] The Secretariat will consider submissions from any person, non-governmental organization, or association that asserts that a country has failed to effectively enforce its environmental law. The core of the commission, the Secretariat has the ability to conduct research and compile information, and is authorized to channel noncompliance reports.

The Joint Public Advisory Committee will include five members of the public from each country. The Joint Committee will advise the Council and provide technical, scientific and other information to the Secretariat. It will include participation from citizens and NGOs.

The Commission for Environmental Cooperation established a complex process through which complaints by any party can ultimately result in a monetary penalty. Any party may request an arbitral panel if the Council cannot resolve a party's alleged persistent pattern of failure to effectively enforce an environmental law relating to a situation involving the production of goods or services traded between the parties. If the panel finds that indeed a persistent failure to enforce environmental law has occurred, the parties have a sixty-day time frame to agree on a mutually satisfactory action plan to remedy the nonenforcement. If no action plan is agreed upon, then within 60 to 120 days the panel may reconvene and make a determination on the imposition of monetary penalty against the party complained against. In the event that Mexico or the United States[33] fails to pay the monetary fine or continues to violate its respective environmental law, that country is liable to the suspension of NAFTA benefits based on the amount of the assessment.

ON THE PATH TO BILATERAL LABOR COOPERATION

The bilateral relationship between the United States and Mexico on labor related issues has been very recent. Prior to the 1990s, bilateral labor relations had been relegated to international multilateral accords negotiated in the International Labor Organization (ILO). During the Carter administration, secretary of labor Ray Marshall concocted a short lived cooperation project that proposed to exchange information on labor statistics and related topics. Apparently, however, this endeavor never fully crystallized.[34] Therefore, from the Carter administration up to the Bush years, discussion of labor issues was practically nil. The 1991 Memorandum of Understanding (MOU) was the first agreement that established the interest of both nations in promoting the rights of workers to a better standard of living and a safe occupation. Among the designated areas of future cooperation were safety and health, conflict resolution proceedings, social security systems, labor statistics, and productivity and quality. An Agreement was also reached to promote joint ventures, information exchanges on statistics, procedures and rules, and delegation exchanges to study the labor system in each country.

On August 13, 1993, the ministers of the three countries reached an understanding on the North American Agreement on Labor Cooperation (NAALC). The intention of the Agreement is to pursue a set of general objectives which aim at complementing the NAFTA by promoting the improvement of working conditions and living standards in all three countries. The Agreement addresses a broad range of common labor areas. As in the Environmental Agreement, the most important aspect of the NAALC centers on the obligation of each party to ensure the enforcement of its domestic labor laws. In its preamble and principles, the Agreement stipulates that each party commits itself, in accordance with its domestic laws, to promote the following principles: the freedom of association, the right to bargain collectively, the right to strike, prohibition of forced labor, minimum employment standards, prevention of occupational accidents, and protection of migrant workers. It also provides mechanisms to permit problem-solving consultations, enables the Parties to initiate evaluations of patterns of practice by independent community of experts, and in certain cases allows for dispute settlement procedures. The main objectives of the Agreement are to improve working conditions and living standards in the region, to promote the compliance with the labor laws of each country, and to exchange and publish information on labor issues and on the laws, institutions and standards of each nation, in order to enhance mutual understanding.

The Commission, created to facilitate the achievement of the objectives put forth by the Agreement, is composed of the Ministerial Council, the International Coordinating Secretariat, and the National Administrative Offices (NAOs). The Ministerial Council consists of the labor ministers from the three North American countries. Its task is to supervise the implementation of the Agreement, including the work of the International Coordinating Secretariat. It may also create working groups and committees they deem appropriate to further the objectives of the Agreement.

The International Coordinating Secretariat (ICS) acts under the direction of the Ministerial Council.[35] Its duty is to carry out the day-to-day work of the Commission. It is responsible for assisting the Council in its work, for gathering and periodically publishing information on labor matters in Canada, Mexico and the United States, for planning and coordinating cooperative activities, and for supporting any working groups or evaluation committees established by the Ministerial Council. The ICS will be headed by an Executive Director appointed by consensus of the parties for a fixed term, and the Executive Director will appoint the staff.

National Administrative Offices (NAOs) are established by each country to serve as the points of contact to facilitate the exchange of information between parties. For instance, they will provide information on domestic law and practice, receive public communications, conduct preliminary reviews, and promote the exchange of information relevant to the Agreement. Each nation has the autonomy to design and designate its own NAO.

If the Council is unable to resolve a dispute involving a party's alleged persistent pattern of failure to effectively enforce labor laws with respect to health and safety, child labor, or minimum wage, any party can request an arbitral panel by a two-thirds vote of the Council. The panel may seek information and technical advice from any person or body that it deems appropriate. If the panel concludes that persistent failure has indeed occurred, there is a sixty-day period in which parties can agree on a mutually satisfactory remedy. If there is no agreed action plan, then within 60 to 120 days, the panel may impose a monetary fine against the country not in compliance. If the country fails to pay or continues to fail to enforce labor law with respect to health and safety, child labor and minimum wage, it is liable to ongoing enforcement actions. In the case of Mexico and the United States, the complaining party or parties may suspend NAFTA benefits based on the amount of the assessment.

FINAL CONSIDERATIONS

The agreements and commissions on labor and environmental cooperation, devised by the parallel accords, can represent important mechanisms for binational an trinational collaboration. The agreements establish institutions with specific rules and norms. They contain dispute settlement procedures with limited but real enforcement capabilities. The installment of National Administrative Offices in the case of labor, and an environmental Joint Public Advisory Committee, guarantees a constant interaction among officials from the three nations.[36]

The structure and content of the environmental and labor commissions are designed to expand cooperation among the nations of North America. These commissions establish direct lines for information exchanges. The rules and dispute resolution mechanisms provide clear guidelines that can ease the management of conflictual situations. In short, it can be expected that the commissions will augment cooperative endeavors, by providing information to the decision makers involved in the issue area, and reducing uncertainty in the day to day handling of bilateral affairs.

Although the institutionalization of bilateral environment and labor affairs can facilitate the development of cooperation, a few caveats must be explored. The successful development of the North American Agreement on Labor Cooperation (NAALC) and the North American Agreement on Environmental Cooperation (NAAEC) will depend to a large degree on whether NAFTA effectively delivers economic benefits, and as well whether it deepens the economic integration in the region. A high and positive correlation exist between economic integration and the role played by the parallel accords. NAALC and NAAEC tasks will expand only if integration becomes a reality; a reduction of bilateral economic exchanges will diminish the scope of action of the parallel agreements.

The domestic component of the three nations is also an important variable. A separation of Quebec from the rest of Canada would change the dynamic of NAFTA, making the francophone province a fourth actor. Moreover, as the Mexican experience of 1994 and 1995 revealed, political destabilization in Mexico, or in any of the countries of the region, could translate into neglect of the Agreements and NAFTA in general, as attention and efforts are redirected to deal with the domestic dilemmas.

This chapter has argued that the commissions can aid the development of cooperation by offering a forum where conflicts can be discussed and eventually solved. In the debate on the amount of institutionalization, however, there are some detractors. Not all analysts agree that institutionalization will have a positive impact. Some analysts maintain that the commissions will slow down cooperative efforts by introducing more actors and agencies onto the scene. For example, a larger number of bureaucrats and officers will never be able to accomplish joint projects in the efficient manner that a one-to-one interaction between government officials can achieve. Although this reasoning contains some truth, a cooperative framework of this kind is subordinated to the type of relationship achieved by the governmental officials. That is, cooperation depends on specific individuals, while a formalized structure can more easily withstand modifications of individuals and administrations.

The exploration of the possible effects of the commissions on future bilateral cooperation has to be understood as an introductory exercise.

The commissions, which officially began work on January 1, 1994, are in an embryonic stage and are still in thc process of being set up. Any attempt at determining their effect on future U.S.-Mexican cooperation, collaboration and coordination can be made only with the understanding that it constitutes a preliminary appraisal. Nevertheless, it is important to trace the development of the commissions set up by the agreements, in an effort to determine the role of international institutions on cooperative efforts between Mexico and the United States.

NOTES

1. Interview with Robert Zoellick, Washington, D.C., April 1994.

2. See Pedro Aspe, *El Camino Mexicano de la Transformación Economica* (Mexico, D.F.: Fondo de Cultura Económica, 1993).

3. A good example of this new trend is the transformation of the Mexican foreign investment code, which translated into an increase of U.S. foreign investment. In 1989 the amount of direct U.S. foreign investment was $1,813 millions, and in 1990 this had increased to $2,308 millions. Pacific Basin Economic Council, *Mexico Investment Handbook*, pp. 140-143.

4. See Rolando Cordera and Carlos Tello, eds., *Mexico Disputa por la Nacion* (Mexico, D.F.: Siglo XXI, 1981).

5. For Texas the relation with Mexico has always been of utmost importance, since half of U.S.-Mexican trade flows through this state.

6. See William Orme, Jr., *Continental Shift Free Trade and the New North America* (Washington D.C.: Washington Post Co., 1993).

7. It is important to bear in mind that although this chapter covers only the background and effects of labor and environmental cooperation in U.S.-Mexican relations, the NAALC and the NAAEC are trilateral agreements comprising the United States, Canada, and Mexico.

8. For an analysis of NGOs and bilateral relations, see Cathryn Thorp, "The Politics of Free Trade and the Dynamics of Cross-Border Coalitions in U.S.-Mexican Relations," *Columbia Journal of World Business* 26, no. 11 (Summer 1991): 12-26.

9. The argument of the applicability of common interest as a precondition is made in Robert Keohane, *After Hegemony, Cooperation and Discord in the World Political Economy* (Princeton: Princeton University Press, 1984); and *International Institutions and State Power* (Boulder, Colo.: Westview Press, 1989).

10. See Blanca Torres, ed., *Interdependencia ¿Un Enfoque Util para el Análisis de las Relaciones Mexico-Estados Unidos?* (Mexico, D.F.: Colmex, 1990).

11. Robert Keohane, *International Institutions and State Power*, p. 3.

12. Ibid, pp. 2-4.

13. Ibid., p. 2.

14. Douglass C. North, in *Institutions, Institutional Change, and Economic Performance* (Cambridge: Cambridge University Press, 1991), p. 4, argues that the effect of institutions on economic performance is to reduce uncertainty by establishing a stable (not necessarily efficient) structure of human interactions.

15. It was enforcement and not the Mexican laws themselves that presented the problem for the environmental NGOs. The 1988 Mexican *Ley de Equilibrio Ecologico y Proteccion Ambiental* was in some respects even stricter than U.S. laws, by requesting an environmental impact assessment (EIA) for all public and private funded projects dealing with toxic waste.

16. The environmental groups supporting the four provisions were: National Wildlife Federation (NWF), National Resources Defense Council (NRDC), Environmental Defense Fund (EDF), and National Audubon Society (NAS). It is important to make a distinction among the different U.S. environmental groups as they are far from being a monolithic force, even if they are usually perceived this way. Christopher Bosso indicates that the environmental movement has transformed itself throughout time into a heterogeneous community of actors, ideologies, and approaches. According to this author, the environmental movement has become divided into three distinct groupings: the "mainstream" environmental groups that have become pragmatists and hence inside players oriented to obtaining acceptable compromises; the "greens" who shun institutional approaches, focusing more on changing societal values; and the "grass root" groups that focus on narrow localized issues. The mainstream groups have become important Washington actors, and obtaining their stamp of approval was a necessity for NAFTA to be passed in Congress. See Christopher Bosso, "Adaptation and Change in the Environmental Movement," in Carl Horn, Donald Baumer, and William Gormley, eds., *Politics and Public Policy* (Washington D.C.: Congressional Quarterly, 1991), pp. 151-176.

17. As written law, current labor standards in Mexico are comparable to or even exceed those in the United States. The Mexican labor laws contain elaborate guidelines on collective bargaining, the right to strike, rights regarding dismissal, an eight hour day, housing benefits, vacations, profit sharing, minimum wage, social security benefits, child care, and health services. As of January 1991, Mexico had also ratified seventy-two International Labor Organization (ILO) conventions dealing with worker

health and safety standards, whereas the United States has ratified only eleven. Robert Pastor concedes that a comparison of Mexican, Canadian and U.S. labor laws suggests that U.S. labor unions would benefit the most from a harmonization of standards. Robert Pastor, "NAFTA as the Center of an Integration Process: The Nontrade Issues," in Nora Lustig, Barry D. Bosworth and Robert Z. Lawrence, eds., *North American Free Trade: Assessing the Impact* (Washington D.C.: The Brookings Institution, 1992), p. 187.

18. As of December 1990, the average manufacturing sector cash wage including fringe benefits was said to be only $1.23 per hour. The comparable figure for *maquiladora* workers was $1.26 per hour. This means that the Mexican industrial wage is about one-eleventh of the U.S. level. U.S. Department of Labor, Bureau of International Labor Affairs.

19. Declaration of the Executive Council of the AFL-CIO on the NAFTA, in *Trabajo* no. 5-6 (Mexico, D.F.: UAM Iztapalapa, 1991).

20. Keith Bradsher, "Fund to Move Companies to Mexico," *The New York Times*, February 17, 1993, p. C1.

21. The well known "sucking sound" argument presented by Ross Perot came to represent the fears of many U.S. workers.

22. See Robert Pastor, "NAFTA as the Center of an Integration Process: The Nontrade Issues," in Nora Lustig, Barry D. Bosworth and Robert Z. Lawrence, eds., *North American Free Trade: Assessing the Impact* (Washington, D.C.: Brookings Institution, 1992).

23. The environmental movement is not, of course, monolithic. While some groups, such as the National Wildlife Federation, supported the fast track negotiating authority after President Bush assured them he would include environmental considerations, the Sierra Club and Friends of the Earth maintained their opposition to the fast track and to NAFTA in general.

24. The proposal for a North American Commission for the Environment (NACE) was one of the main promises made by President Bush in his May 1 "Action Plan" that pledged to address environmental issues both in the NAFTA text and through bilateral and trilateral cooperative efforts. The May Action Plan was a response to a letter sent by Chairman Rostenkowski and Senator Bentsen indicating that, to secure fast track, the Administration would have to commit to decisive measures to confront the environmental and labor concerns. The Action Plan addressed environmental protection in three ways: first, through explicit NAFTA provisions; second, by strongly supporting the Border Environmental Plan; and finally, through bilateral and trilateral arrangements including a North American Commission on the Environment (NACE). It addressed labor concerns through explicit NAFTA provisions, a formal binational cooperation program with Mexico, and a new job training program.

25. William A. Orme, Jr., *Continental Shift, Free Trade and the New North America* (Washington, D.C.: Washington Post Co., 1993), p. 112.

26. In a speech at the University of North Carolina on October 4, 1992, Bill Clinton finally endorsed the free trade agreement with Mexico on the following terms: "I came here to tell you why I support the North American Free Trade Agreement. If it is done right, it will create jobs in the United States and Mexico. If you look at the experience of the *maquiladora* plants there is cause for concern. We can see clearly there that labor standards have been regularly violated, and environmental standards are often ignored... As president I will seek to address the deficiencies of the NAFTA through supplemental agreements with the Canadian and the Mexican governments. I will not sign legislation implementing the NAFTA until we have reached additional agreements to protect America's vital interests." Excerpts from Governor Bill Clinton's speech at North Carolina State University, October 4, 1992. Taken from Rod Dobell and Michael Neufeld, eds., *Beyond NAFTA: The Western Hemisphere Interface*, The North American Institute (Lantzville, British Columbia: Oolichan Books, 1993), pp. 183-194.

27. On May 4, 1993, seven of the largest environmental NGOs submitted a proposal for a side agreement, which they expressed, was essential for their support of the final NAFTA text. Their most pressing demand was the creation of a Commission with meaningful responsibilities and public participation.

28. The International Boundary Commission was established in 1889 to deal with the problems generated by the changing riverbeds of the Colorado and Bravo rivers. In 1944, the Commission was renamed the International Boundary and Water Commission (IBWC), and its responsibilities were extended to include problems of quality, conservation and utilization of water resources in the border region.

29. The La Paz Agreements coordinators were Sergio Reyes Lujan, Undersecretary of Ecology in Mexico, and Timothy Atkeson, Assistant Administrator of International Activities of the Environmental Protection Agency (EPA). In terms of bureaucratic development, this was an important step, because it clearly specified roles in the ministries of both countries.

30. For a detailed account of the Integrated Border Environmental Plan, see Jan Gilbreath Rich, "Planning the Border's Future: The Mexican-U.S Integrated Border Environmental Plan," Mexican Policy Studies Program (Austin: University of Texas, March 1992).

31. The "teeth" that were being demanded consisted of provisions that could make enforcement a real issue. "Goodwill" agreements, such as the Border Environmental Plan, were not respected because they introduced only moral discipline into the accord.

32. The Secretariat of the Commission for Environmental Commission is located in Montreal, Canada and is headed by Victor Lichtinger, a Mexican lawyer.

33. In the case of Canada the Commission, on the request of the complainant, collects the monetary penalty and enforces an action plan in summary proceedings before a Canadian court of competent jurisdiction.

34. In an interview with John Vincent of the U.S. Department of Labor, he remarked that this labor exchange program was the only cooperation project which he could recall prior to the 1990's.

35. The ICS is located in Dallas, Texas, and the Director, John McKinnery, is a Canadian citizen.

36. Jorge Perez Lopez, interim director of the U.S. National Administrative Office (NAO), remarked that the communication lines between himself and the first Mexican NAO Director, Ambassador Jorge Casellas, are constant, consisting of almost daily telephone calls to review the daily issues of the NAOs. Personal interview, Department of Labor, Washington D.C., August 1994.

7

Next Steps: Policy Options After NAFTA

Sidney Weintraub

Now that the North American Free Trade Agreement (NAFTA) is in effect, the three member countries have a number of options from which to choose for its further development. The main ones are the following:

1. Delay expansion to new members in order to give the NAFTA countries time to develop their modus operandi, particularly in those areas not well defined in the underlying agreement. These include procedures for setting industrial, environmental, safety, sanitary, and other standards, and how advance consultation should work when new regulations are being considered in any of the three countries or major policy changes are contemplated that could affect other members. This option may be chosen by default as the U.S. Congress delays or possibly even refuses to extend fast-track negotiating authority.

2. Be prepared to negotiate the adherence of Chile, the Latin American country most ready to accept the undertakings of NAFTA. In theory this need not await fast-track authority. But if this option is chosen, the agreement with Chile will surely become the model for other applicants; consequently, the terms of admission required for Chile—particularly if they weaken any of the understandings reached in NAFTA itself—will signal what the NAFTA countries have in mind regarding the intensity of their future integration activities.

3. NAFTA, operating as a unit, can negotiate either with individual countries for their adherence or, alternatively, insist that other subregional groupings in the Western Hemisphere also negotiate as a unit. A separate negotiation with Chile would weaken any insistence on subregion-to-subregion negotiation, but not necessary preclude it,

because Chile is not a member of any subregional integration arrangement. By contrast, a separate NAFTA negotiation with, say, Argentina or Colombia, which are members of other subregional groupings, would destroy the ability to insist on subregion-to-subregion negotiations for accession to NAFTA.

4. The United States, if it wishes to obtain concessions from applicant countries that go beyond what was achieved in NAFTA, could engage in bilateral negotiations instead of accession to NAFTA. The AFL-CIO has indicated its preference for this approach in negotiations with Chile, as a way to obtain more demanding conditions on labor matters than exist in NAFTA or its side agreement on labor cooperation. Here again, Chile could serve as a model for future negotiations. Neither Chile nor Mexico could make a strong argument against this approach because they already have a separate bilateral free-trade agreement. Canada could legitimately object on the grounds that this approach revives the reality of hub-and-spoke integration, and if the United States chooses this option, Canada would certainly then seek to protect itself by its own bilateral agreement with Chile and with any other countries with which the United States concludes bilateral agreements. Canada may even embark on its own competitive bilateralism if the United States leads the way.

5. Accession to NAFTA under any of the options listed above need not be limited to countries in the Western Hemisphere. The countries whose economies are growing most rapidly are in East Asia, and free-trade agreements with these countries, either individually or by region-to-region negotiations, are possible. So are bilateral agreements with East Asian countries by any of the three NAFTA members.

6. Finally, because widening of NAFTA to additional countries will take time, agreements less ambitious than NAFTA may be necessary to prevent trade and investment diversion that could harm other countries in the Western Hemisphere. These could take a variety of forms, from the most rudimentary, such as the framework agreements that already exist, to more elaborate free-trade agreements less comprehensive than NAFTA.

Decisions will be needed in the near future on which option (or options) to choose. These decisions will be needed in the United States, the other NAFTA countries, other countries in this hemisphere, and potentially in Asia. The decisions made will have much influence on trading patterns of all these countries and on the institutional machinery for carrying them out.

This chapter examines the implications of the various options and makes a number of policy suggestions.

ANALYSIS OF THE OPTIONS

Define NAFTA First, Then Expand Membership

The argument for this approach is that although NAFTA provides a framework for comprehensive economic integration, it does not assure this outcome. The corollary to this position is that optimal benefits from economic integration come not merely from the elimination of border barriers or even from encouraging capital to flow to those locations where its return is greatest, but rather from dealing comprehensively with related policies such as those affecting dispute settlement, regulatory activity, internal as well as external competition, and impediments to the free flow of services. The so-called new issues in the Uruguay Round of negotiations in the General Agreement on Tariffs and Trade (GATT)—services, intellectual property, trade-related investment measures, and agricultural protection and subsidies—came to the fore because the traditional border barriers have become less significant in limiting international trade. One of the major successes of NAFTA is that it was able to deal comprehensively with these issues.

The declining importance of border barriers is evident as well in recent proposals and actions affecting international trade. The Economic Commission for Latin America and the Caribbean (ECLAC) now favors what has come to be called "open regionalism," which entails market liberalization, but also stable and transparent rules on a broad array of internal and external policies.[1] The position for which this organization was once best known, that of industrialization through import substitution, was based on high border barriers. Perhaps more telling, four countries of the European Free Trade Association (EFTA) which already have free trade with the European Union (EU)—that is, the absence of most border barriers—have negotiated for entry into the EU, subject to approval in separate national referenda. (They are Austria, Finland, Norway, and Sweden.) These countries also wish to participate in the decision-making on competition issues, setting standards in a variety of fields, designing social policy, and shaping the future monetary system of the EU. The virtual elimination of border barriers is not enough for taking full advantage of economic integration.

The EU (first as the European Economic Community, then as the European Community, and now as the European Union) had its own gradual process of what is generally referred to as "deepening." NAFTA will require its own deepening, different in scope and intent from that of Western Europe but still significant in defining the nature of the integration movement. For example, the following issues must be dealt with in NAFTA:

- Standards must be set for industrial products, the tolerable limits of pesticide residues on edible products, and the weight and size of trucks in cross-border traffic.
- The tens of thousands of pages of new and revised regulations issued in the three countries can alter the balance of benefits that the member countries expected from NAFTA, and some way is needed for each country to penetrate the regulatory processes of the others.
- NAFTA establishes a number of dispute settlement procedures, and these must be institutionalized and then tested in practice.
- The major complaint of Canada in the operation of the Canada-U.S. Free Trade Agreement (CUFTA) has been the way the United States uses anti-dumping and countervailing duty procedures, so some means may be necessary within NAFTA to prevent this form of contingent protection from replacing the now less onerous and more transparent border barriers.
- Because exchange rate swings can swamp the effects of tariff reductions under NAFTA, the central bankers must look at techniques to minimize these shifts.
- NAFTA already has committees and working parties examining customs procedures, rules of origin, agricultural subsidies, rules for providing financial services, and many other matters that transcend the actual level of border restrictions; decisions on these seemingly technical matters can define the extent of the integration that will take place.
- Beyond these committees, two supplementary agreements have been reached among the three countries, on environmental and labor cooperation; the manner in which these will be institutionalized must be worked out.

- Finally, the habit of cooperation that is a promise of NAFTA requires consultation on ancillary issues, such as immigration, which until now have been handled almost purely as internal matters.

Unlike the EU, the member countries of NAFTA do not contemplate monetary or economic union, let alone political union. Nevertheless, a deepening process in NAFTA does imply some diminution of sovereignty—if that is defined as the ability of each country to make its own decisions on economic policy. The word "diminution" may not be the correct one—perhaps the better usage is "sharing of sovereignty." Binding arbitration by panels composed of nonnationals as well as nationals, as contemplated in dealing with countervailing and anti-dumping duty disputes under Chapter 19 of NAFTA, will remove some activities from national courts. The two supplementary agreements envisage that each country is responsible not only to its own nationals for carrying out its own laws and regulations relating to environmental protection and safeguarding workplace standards, but also to a trinational commission. These, for the most part, are modest derogations of sovereignty, but they do change the way these issues are handled.

The derogation of sovereignty will be more substantial if and as techniques are found under which new national regulations are vetted with the other two countries before becoming final.

The United States, in 1993, adopted what was referred to as a blockade to limit the entry of illegal aliens into El Paso, Texas. This entailed substantial use of the Border Patrol. In the process, procedures for legal entries into El Paso were made more burdensome, and this had an adverse effect on cross-border commerce. Fences are going up in many places along the U.S. border with Mexico. U.S. Attorney General Janet Reno announced in February 1994 that some version of the El Paso blockade technique will be proposed more generally along the border. In each case, the original blockade and the proposed extension to other places on the border, there was no advance consultation with Mexico; in each case, the Mexican authorities questioned whether these unilateral actions were in the spirit of NAFTA.[2] Mexican authorities still have misgivings about these U.S. actions, but consultations on new measures are now the norm.

Canada chose the free-trade area rather than a customs union format when it proposed economic integration with the United States. One argument Canadians put forward was that a customs union, under which there is a common external tariff (CET), might have led to raising U.S. tariffs in order to reach an average with the higher Canadian tariff level in setting the CET. The real reason was that Canada was concerned that a customs union would entail more of a political commitment, in that Canada would lose the power to set its own external tariff and have an independent commercial policy.

Yet there will be inexorable pressure for tariffs among the three countries to equalize, particularly for intermediate and capital-goods imports, lest the lowest tariff country become the preferred choice for location of plants requiring imports from outside the NAFTA area. There will even be pressure for tariff equalization for consumer goods. Canada, in early 1994, found it necessary to lower cigarette taxes in order to reduce widespread smuggling from the United States, where taxes were about one-fifth as high.[3] This was a sin tax, a revenue measure, but the principle would be the same were it a border tariff. Try as it will to maintain its sovereign power to set its own tariffs against countries that are not members of NAFTA, the exercise is doomed to fail (or, at best, to be diluted) by the existence of NAFTA. This statement applies to all three countries of NAFTA, not just Canada.

NAFTA has the potential to become a form of "strong" integration going beyond the elimination of border barriers, but also the possibility to be a "weak" integration arrangement concentrating on trade and investment preferences while otherwise catering to the most potent protectionist interests in the three countries. As the most powerful country, the actions of the United States are most crucial for the eventual development of the arrangement. If anti-dumping and countervailing duty actions continue to proliferate as they have in recent years, little will have been accomplished by using this form of contingent protection to substitute for tariffs and for explicit quotas and other nontariff measures. Regulations can be used to encourage a North American mentality or, alternatively, to favor national interests. If customs procedures are made complex and dilatory, this would discourage cross-border co-production to meet just-in-time inventory techniques.

Or, to focus not on NAFTA as such but on the cooperative spirit necessary to make it work, if any of the countries acts without prior consultation on issues of vital importance to the other countries, this could doom NAFTA from the outset. The immigration issue is the most salient recent example of this, but others can emerge, such as conflict on dealing with traffic in narcotics.

The case for pursuing the first option—to delay widening NAFTA until a greater degree of deepening has taken place within North America—is to avoid the distraction of outside negotiations with countries that are not geographically contiguous. These noncontiguous countries do not have the same border environment relations as the United States has with its two neighbors, the relationship of their physical infrastructure (roads, railways, sewage facilities, water use) with the NAFTA region is largely irrelevant, and the introduction of different legal and regulatory procedures before the three countries of North American have worked out their arrangements could destroy any ability to achieve strong integration.

The European experience is that the benefits of economic integration are maximized when this goes beyond dealing with the most evident border barriers. Strong integration has not yet been achieved in North America. Until more progress is made on this score, my view is that the NAFTA countries would be well advised to hold off new entries—certainly hold off new entries other than possibly Chile, where a commitment seems to have been made—until there is more deepening in NAFTA itself. This may be unnecessary advice. The political situation in the United States and the objective economic scene in Latin American and Caribbean (LAC) countries may make expansion of NAFTA impossible in the near future in any event. This may not be a bad outcome.

Proceed with Negotiation for Accession of Chile

Chile is the only country in the LAC region for which two conditions apply: it has taken the necessary economic restructuring measures that make it able to accede to NAFTA with only a short transition before fully undertaking the main commitments of the agreement; and, at the same time, it is not a member of any subregional economic grouping. Chile was prepared to negotiate a free-trade agreement with the United States even as Mexico was doing so, but was held off on the grounds that the U.S. Congress wanted only one such comprehensive negotiation at that time.

Free-trade negotiations with Chile would probably present fewer political problems in the United States than did the negotiations with Mexico. Chile sends few low-wage manufactured goods to the United States. Imports of manufactured goods from Chile in 1992 were only $634 million, compared with $27 billion from Mexico.[4] Because of distance, Chile is not a prime location for co-production in the manner of Mexico or the Caribbean; Chile offers little incentive for production of industrial inputs for U.S. firms using just-in-time inventory management.

This does not mean there would be no negotiating problems. U.S. wine producers would likely resist free entry of Chilean wines. The same is true for U.S. salmon fishermen. Chilean fruits and vegetables have the advantage of coming to the U.S. market at a different season from U.S. products, and therefore might not arouse much protectionist sentiment. In a negotiation, the United States undoubtedly would expect Chile to remove some of the technical impediments to foreign direct investment and limitations on capital repatriation, and to strengthen protection of intellectual property, although none of these issues is likely to present insurmountable problems.[5]

Yet these very advantages of negotiating with Chile point up some of the disadvantages for the United States. Chile is a small country with a modest market. Total U.S. exports to Chile in 1992 were less than $2.5 billion; U.S. exports to Mexico in 1992 were more than $40 billion.[6] Chile in and of itself is therefore not very interesting as a market for U.S. products. Beyond that, the United States does not dominate Chile's trade, either imports or exports, in the same way it does Mexico's. In recent years, Chile has traded more with Japan and the European Union than with the United States. Because it is not a member of any subregional economic group, U.S. and other corporations would obtain no tariff advantage when producing in Chile for export to other countries in the LAC region. This may change if Chile is able to negotiate a free-trade arrangement with the four countries of the Southern Common Market (MERCOSUR), as it intends to do.

The reasons for supporting Chilean accession to NAFTA are thus twofold: it would signal U.S. sincerity in wanting to expand free trade throughout the Western Hemisphere, and Chile is the only country now fully ready for accession; and the agreement with Chile could establish a substantive pattern for subsequent accession negotiations. Put slightly differently, a negotiation with Chile could make it clear that the NAFTA countries have no intention of weakening their arrangement to accommodate potential new entrants. This, I think, is the most solid substantive reason for supporting Chilean accession to NAFTA.

Accession by Countries or by Subregions

Many Latin American countries are looking for free trade—for better market access—wherever and with whomever they can get it. Thus Mexico, in addition to joining NAFTA, signed much less comprehensive free-trade agreements with Chile, Costa Rica, Bolivia, and jointly with Colombia and Venezuela (the so-called G-3). Colombia and Venezuela are members of the Andean Group (which also includes Bolivia, Ecuador, and Peru). Argentina, a member of MERCOSUR (which also includes Brazil, Paraguay, and Uruguay), has indicated its desire to accede to NAFTA, although not necessarily immediately. Costa Rica, a member of the Central American Common Market (CACM)—which also includes El Salvador, Guatemala, Honduras, and Nicaragua—made overtures for acceding to NAFTA. So did Jamaica, a member of the Caribbean Common Market (CARICOM), which includes a number of English-speaking countries in the Caribbean.

The LAC region is already mishmash of integration groupings and separate bilateral agreements, and double loyalties of individual countries can only complicate trade arrangements. These complications include varying tariff levels and nontariff measures, and different degrees of trade preferences, rules of origin, customs clearance arrangements, and dispute settlement procedures.

Much more serious than complexity, however, is that these defections from the subregions are likely to prejudice any deepening of those agreements. This is happening even as intra-Latin American exports of manufactured products are growing. These exports amount to about one-fourth of total LAC exports of manufactures, about half the proportion that goes to the United States.[7] The consequences of defection are perhaps more serious, in that development attention is thereby diverted from thinking regionally to looking north to the United States. One of the defects of earlier efforts at economic integration in Latin America was the inadequacy of transportation and communication facilities within the subregions. This is still largely the case. Miami is still the main intermediary point for travel between Caribbean countries.

Should the United States—should the three NAFTA countries—care if South America looks north more than it searches subregionally for economic linkages? Yes, if by looking north these countries prejudice their long-term economic development; no, if looking north is the best path to development. There are various views on this within the subregions. The countries defecting to NAFTA apparently think they can have it both ways, simultaneous integration subregionally and with North America. The president of Uruguay sees it differently: "The integration movement in Latin America must be modular and step by step. When you think of MERCOSUR, it is made real by geography."[8]

My view is that the three NAFTA countries should resist country-by-country applications for accession. Not only would this prejudice the deepening of North American integration, but it also would damage the deepening within subregional groupings. If any individual country from an existing subregional grouping is admitted to NAFTA, there is then no basis for not entertaining applications from all other countries in that grouping. From the U.S. perspective, few of these individual countries are substantial markets, whereas their subregions are more interesting both for exports and for bases of production.[9] The more rapidly their economies grow, the more interesting the subregions are in an economic sense. I agree with the sentiment of Uruguay's president that Western Hemisphere economic integration is best achieved in modules, bloc by bloc, and not by country by country, adherence to NAFTA.

Widening by Accession to NAFTA or Bilaterally

When Mexico requested negotiations with the United States for a free-trade agreement, one reason Canada felt constrained to join the process was to prevent the emergence of hub-and-spoke economic integration. The term refers to the United States (or any country) being the hub country that concludes free-trade agreements with a number of countries (the spokes) which do not have free trade with each other. The economics of such an arrangement are that only the hub country enjoys free entry of its goods into all the spoke countries, whereas they benefit only from free trade with the hub. Under these circumstances, the hub country is the preferred location for new investment.[10]

If the United States were to negotiate a bilateral free-trade agreement with Chile, this would be a revival of hub-and-spoke integration. Canada, in these circumstances, would surely feel deceived. It could protect itself by signing its own bilateral free-trade agreement with Chile, adding much complexity to the trading arrangements. If Chile's bilateral agreement were only the first of many for the United States, the complexity would soon compound itself. Not only would Canada find it necessary to reach its own separate bilaterals, but so would Mexico and Chile, and so on ad infinitum. Any country that left itself only as a spoke would be disadvantaged in its market access to other countries and in attracting investment. The outcome would be analogous to a never-ending chain letter as each new bilateral spawned two, three, four, or more other bilaterals. Like a chain letter, the process would eventually collapse of its own weight.

This is a bad idea. The motivation of the AFL-CIO is to maximize its leverage in obtaining improved working conditions as part of trade agreements. This effort has a long history in the GATT, in U.S. grants of tariff preferences to developing countries, and most recently in NAFTA. Yet it would be hard to justify compromising the trading system in this hemisphere—and the potential this provides for improved economic growth—to achieve the kind of self-defeating complexity endless bilateral agreements would generate.

Extra-Hemispheric Free-Trade Agreements

Nothing in the accession article of NAFTA or the enabling legislation putting it into effect limits membership to countries in the Western Hemisphere. Widening in this hemisphere has dominated the discussion because that is the way the issue was first presented when President Bush's Enterprise for the Americas initiative suggested the desirability of constructing a Western Hemisphere Free Trade Area (WHFTA).

There is much support for widening to Asia. Asian economic growth rates are higher than those in the LAC countries. In sheer value terms, Asia is a bigger market for U.S. exports than the Western Hemisphere. If there is to be free trade, why not focus on the most interesting markets?[11] There is also a budding regional integration movement in Southeast Asia, the ASEAN Free Trade Area (AFTA), although this is less advanced than many of the subregional arrangements in the Western Hemisphere.

Yet the issue is more complex than simply looking at the size of economies. The United States is the dominant exporter to the LAC region. Although there are differences among countries, the United States provides about 40 percent of the region's imports. Thus, as the region grows, the marginal share of the United States in the imports generated is substantial. U.S. exports to LAC countries grew by more than 19 percent in nominal dollar terms in 1991-92.[12]

By contrast, the United States typically provides around 20 percent of the imports of countries in Asia, and the same level of economic growth there as in the LAC region provides less of a marginal stimulus for U.S. exports. It takes more than twice as much growth in Asia as in the LAC region to provide the same marginal stimulus for U.S. exports. The principal developed country exporter to Asian countries is Japan. Japan's stake in Asia's economic growth is comparable to the U.S. stake in LAC growth. Japan did much better than the United States in its exports to developing countries in its region during the 1980s because the Asian countries where its primary markets are located grew at a faster rate than did the LAC countries.

A U.S. attempt to develop free-trade agreements with Asian countries, whether bilaterally or through accession to NAFTA, would have the earmarks of a declaration of trade war against Japan. The United States would be seen as seeking preferential treatment in Japan's sphere of trade influence, and this would provoke a reaction. The likely reaction would be comparable to how the United States would have responded had Japan, before NAFTA, suggested a free-trade agreement with Mexico.

Trade shares are not static. There is no reason why Japan—or the EU—should not seek to build its market share in the LAC region, or the United States in the Asian and European regions. These efforts are already taking place on both continents. The techniques are more local production in the region, more co-production, more direct investment, better export financing, more servicing of products, strategic alliances, and so on. These traditional techniques do not arouse the animosity that preferential agreements would stimulate.

My recommendation is that the United States, to the extent that it wishes to widen NAFTA, stick with the LAC region—at least for now—and seek further penetration of the Asian region by traditional methods.

Interim Measures

NAFTA is in existence and its provisions are being carried out. Widening to other LAC countries, even if it takes place, will take time. There is a legitimate question about what the LAC countries and the three NAFTA countries—particularly the United States—can and should do in the interim.

The potential for trade and investment diversion as a consequence of NAFTA has not been completely examined. The preliminary indication is that diversion might be greatest for countries in Central America and the Caribbean, many of which rely heavily—50 percent or more—on the U.S. market. The danger of diversion scales down for countries which rely less heavily on the U.S. market. Venezuela and Colombia tend to send between 40 and 50 percent of their merchandise exports to the United States; this proportion falls to 10 to 20 percent for the two Southern Cone countries, Chile and Argentina. Ironically, it is the latter two that have been the most ardent applicants for accession to NAFTA, although that of Argentina seems to be diminishing. They are obviously looking to the potential of attracting new investment and stimulating future exports. Thus, the extent of trade reliance on the United States is not a complete guide in setting priorities for widening NAFTA.

Reliance on the U.S. market is inadequate in assessing potential trade diversion in other respects as well. Venezuelan oil and Colombian coffee exports to the United States will not be affected by NAFTA preferences. The commodity breakdown of trade must be examined. Most countries in Central America and the Caribbean benefit from preferences under the Caribbean Basin Initiative (CBI). NAFTA, to a great extent, simply encourages a level playing field for treatment of Mexican and CBI imports into the U.S. market. In some respects, NAFTA will give better treatment to Mexico than is enjoyed under the CBI—sugar is a potential example of this, as is the textile and apparel sector. In other respects, CBI benefits are superior to those of NAFTA—the less strict rule of origin in the CBI compared with NAFTA is an example.

The short answer is that we really do not know the extent of trade and investment diversion that NAFTA will cause. The United States—and the other two NAFTA countries—have an obligation to do no harm, or at least as little harm as possible. The first step, therefore, in devising an interim policy is to undertake more comprehensive studies of diversion. The emphasis in these studies should probably be on the CBI countries, not only because of their heavy reliance on the U.S. market but also because this reliance was promoted by U.S. incentives under that program.

Minimizing the harm—that is, minimizing trade and investment diversion—can take a number of forms. One is to accelerate accession to NAFTA, but, as already noted, this could prejudice NAFTA's deepening if done promiscuously. Most of the countries are not prepared to open their markets as required by NAFTA, and for them the idea of accession with a reasonably short transition period and fully reciprocal obligations as complete as those undertaken by the NAFTA countries is not now a possibility. Their internal restructuring would not permit undertaking these obligations at this time. Accelerated accession to NAFTA is thus not a viable interim solution for most LAC countries.

One proposal that has not garnered great support is to provide the CBI countries parity with Mexico where the NAFTA benefits are superior. A variant of this is to provide parity only for those commodities—textile products in particular—that have taken on much greater salience since the onset of the CBI program. This need not be completely nonreciprocal. In exchange for improved benefits for the CBI countries, the United States and the other NAFTA countries could seek such actions as more liberal treatment of foreign investment, freer entry for services, the conclusion of double taxation treaties, and greater protection for intellectual property. Where relevant, such agreements should be on a most-favored-nation (MFN) basis to avoid violation of GATT provisions.

The United States now has framework agreements with LAC countries. These agreements provide forums for negotiation. Something analogous to what is proposed for CBI countries—to reach limited agreements for those commodities whose exports to North America are likely to be compromised by NAFTA—can be considered for LAC countries generally. As with the CBI countries, this treatment can be reciprocal; each of the countries, or groups of countries, have restrictions that could be eased in return, again on an MFN basis in order not to contravene GATT.

Finally, a procedure similar to that of the European Community (today's EU) might be followed. The deepening commitments undertaken by the members of the Community were not demanded of other countries, but nevertheless trade benefits were provided to nonmembers. These varied from free-trade agreements with EFTA countries and Israel, to less than complete free trade but preferential entry, with much reciprocity, with others, such as the Maghrib countries. Preferences are now being worked out with former Communist countries in Eastern Europe.

A series of concentric circles was thus erected.[13] At the core were the Community countries, one layer out were the EFTA countries, then others with less complete agreements. The level of obligations was greatest at the center and weakest at the outer reaches. Similarly, the benefits were greatest at the center. When countries in the outer layers felt they wished to play under the deepened rules of the core countries, and thus have a say in decision-making, they were considered for full membership. Many countries did enter under these circumstances, and other EFTA countries are in the process of negotiating for entry into the EU as this is written.

NAFTA can emulate this pattern. Some countries, while not ready to undertake deepened obligations of the kind described earlier, may be ready for free trade with NAFTA in the sense of eliminating border and for some other barriers, and undertaking obligations in such fields as trade in services, investment, and protection of intellectual property. Other countries may not be able to go that far, and less comprehensive limited agreements, such as those contemplated with CBI countries, can be considered.

I believe that such an approach is possible and can be carried out consistent with U.S. GATT obligations. This would be a technique for minimizing harm to nonmembers of NAFTA without compromising NAFTA deepening. This approach, if adopted, should be combined with suggestions made earlier that it would be preferable to negotiate these agreements with other subregional groupings rather than individual countries, and to limit them for the time being to the Western Hemisphere.

CONCLUSIONS

The choices that are made now will determine much about both the substance and the architecture of Western Hemisphere economic relations. The churning now taking place in the hemisphere revolves around fundamental issues. These include both national and subregional development policies and the role that trade should play. The shedding of one paradigm, that of import-substituting industrialization, and the adoption of a new model of more open markets with a bias toward export promotion, has made this a particularly pregnant period in hemispheric economic history.

The paradigmatic shift in the LAC countries has been accompanied by one in North America. The United States shed its almost sole reliance on multilateral trade negotiations in favor of a regional-multilateral mixture. Both Canada and Mexico discarded their reluctance to enter into a preferential trading relationship with the United States. This regionalism in North America comes at a time when the LAC countries are considering what ECLAC refers to as "open regionalism," that is, promotion of subregional and eventually even hemispheric economic integration behind low rather than high border barriers.

This is the context in which the kinds of decisions discussed in this chapter must be made. My recommendations on the various issues that must be decided are the following:

1. NAFTA should give itself time to deepen, to institutionalize its accomplishments, before embarking on wholesale expansion to other countries in the hemisphere that are not able or prepared to undertake the obligations entailed in a deepened NAFTA. The prospective economic benefits of NAFTA are substantially greater under a "strong" than under a "weak" integration that is designed primarily to exploit tariff, nontariff, and investment preferences.

2. Chile may be prepared to undertake these obligations, and widening of membership to Chile need not compromise NAFTA's deepening. By itself, however, Chile is only marginally attractive as a market. The terms of its accession, however, can form the template

for future accessions; and if the terms weaken the potential for NAFTA to deepen in ways described in this chapter, it would be wiser not to admit Chile.

3. Other than Chile, which is not a member of any subregional integration grouping, economic integration negotiations are best carried out by subregions, bloc to bloc, that is NAFTA and MERCOSUR, NAFTA and CACM, NAFTA and the Andean Group, NAFTA and CARICOM. The signal this would give is that the subregional deepening in the LAC area has its own validity, and the hemisphere would be strongest if subregional arrangements gained strength.

4. Just as it would be less than optimal for members of LAC subregional groupings to break ranks, so would it be most unwise for the United States to break ranks with its NAFTA partners and negotiate bilateral free-trade agreements with other countries. Mexico has entered into bilateral (or trilateral, in the case of the G-3) free-trade agreements despite its membership in NAFTA. While I think this is unwise, the trade involved is picayune compared with the stakes were the United States to emulate Mexico's action. A new impetus for hub-and-spoke arrangements would set in motion a complex series of negotiations in which each spoke country sought to protect its interests.

5. Widening of NAFTA, to the extent it occurs, is best limited to Western Hemisphere countries at this time. Seeking preferential arrangements with newly industrializing countries in Asia would be an aggressive move of seeking preferential advantage over Japan in the very region in which it dominates trading relationships. The United States would not have reacted calmly had Japan, pre-NAFTA, sought a preferential arrangement with Mexico.

6. The NAFTA countries, particularly the United States, have an obligation to minimize trade and investment diversion affecting other LAC countries. This may require interim arrangements until such time as these countries are willing and able to seek accession to NAFTA. Consideration should thus be given to arrangements less complete and less deep than NAFTA under which NAFTA and other subregional groupings can enter into more limited undertakings. The kinds of concentric circles adopted by the European Community—of deep obligations among the members, free trade without the related deepening with EFTA, reciprocal benefits but less than free trade with

Mediterranean and Eastern European countries—should be examined as potentially applicable in the Western Hemisphere.

NOTES

1. Gert Rosenthal, Executive Secretary of ECLAC, statement on the occasion of the presidential summit of the Rio Group, Santiago, Chile, October 16, 1993.

2. The source for this sentence is a senior official of the Mexican government.

3. Clyde Farnsworth, "Canada Cuts Cigarette Taxes to Fight Smuggling," *New York Times*, February 9, 1994, A3.

4. U.S. Department of Commerce, *U.S. Foreign Trade Highlights 1992* (Washington, D.C.: U.S. Government Printing Office, 1993), 32, 33.

5. See U.S. International Trade Commission, *U.S. Market Access in Latin America: Recent Liberalization Measures and Remaining Barriers (With a Special Case Study on Chile)*, USITC publication 2521 (Washington, D.C.: USITC, 1992), 5-1 to 5-21.

6. U.S. Department of Commerce, *U.S. Foreign Trade Highlights 1992*, 11, 12.

7. Inter-American Development Bank, *Economic and Social Progress in Latin America, 1992 Report* (Baltimore: Johns Hopkins Press for the IDB, 1992), 269. The percentages are for 1990.

8. Stephen Fidler, interview with Luis Alberto Lacalle, *Financial Times*, June 7, 1993, 21.

9. Compared with the more than $40 billion in U.S. exports to Mexico in 1992, the figures for U.S. exports to other LAC countries that year were Brazil, $5.7 billion; Venezuela, $5.4 billion; all of Central America, $5.4 billion; all CARICOM countries, $4 billion; Colombia, $3.3 billion; Argentina, $3.2 billion; and downward from there. Figures from *U.S. Foreign Trade Highlights 1992*, 11-12.

10. The concept and the economics of hub-and-spoke economic integration were first elaborated in Ronald J. Wonnacott, *The Economics of Overlapping Free Trade Areas and the Mexican Challenge* (Toronto and Washington, D.C.: Canadian American Committees, 1991).

11. U.S. merchandise exports to the Asian "tigers" in 1992 were the following: Taiwan, $15 billion; South Korea, close to $15 billion; Singapore, $10 billion; Hong Kong, $9 billion. Exports to the countries of Southeast Asia taken together were $14 billion. Compare these figures with those to the LAC region in note 9, which comes from the same source as this note.

12. U.S. Agency for International Development, *Latin America and the*

Caribbean: Selected Economic and Social Data (Washington, D.C.: USAID, 1993), 138.

13. This approach of concentric circles is described in a paper by Christopher Stevens, "Western Hemisphere Trade Liberalization: The Lessons from European Community Experience," October 1993. Professor Stevens is at the Institute of Development Studies, University of Sussex.

Selected Bibliography

NAFTA

Anderson, Terry (ed.). *NAFTA and the Environment.* San Francisco: Pacific Research Institute for Public Policy, 1993.

Barry, Donald (ed.). *Toward a North American Community? Canada, the United States, and Mexico.* Boulder, Colo.: Westview Press, 1995.

Dean, Judith; Desai, Seema; and Riedel, James. *Trade Policy Reform in Developing Countries Since 1985: A View of the Evidence.* Washington, D.C.: World Bank, 1994.

Doran, Charles F., and Marchildon, Gregory P. (eds.) *The NAFTA Puzzle: Political Parties and Trade in North America.* Boulder, Colo.: Westview Press, 1994.

Globerman, Steven, and Walker, Michael (eds.). *Assessing NAFTA: A Trilateral Analysis.* Vancouver, B.C.: Fraser Institute, 1993.

Grossman, Gene M., and Helpman, Ellanen. *Trade Wars and Trade Talks.* Working Paper no. 4280. Cambridge, Mass.: National Bureau of Economic Research, 1993.

Hufbauer, Gary Clyde, and Schott, Jeffrey J. (eds.). *NAFTA: An Assessment.* Washington, D.C.: Institute for International Economics, 1993.

Krishna, Kala, and Krueger, Anne. *Implementing Free Trade Areas: Rules of Origin and Hidden Protection.* Working Paper no. 4983. Cambridge, Mass.: National Bureau of Economic Research, 1994.

Lemco, Jonathan, and Robson, William (eds.). *Ties Beyond Trade: Labor and Environmental Issues Under the NAFTA*, 1993.

Lustig, Nora; Bosworth, Barry D.; and Lawrence, Robert Z. (eds.). *North American Free Trade: Assessing the Impact.* Washington, D.C.: Brookings Institution, 1992.

Molot, Maureen. *Driving Continentally: National Policies and the North American Auto Industry.* Ottawa: Carlton University Press, 1993.

Morici, Peter. *Trade Talks with Mexico: A Time for Realism.* Washington, D.C.: National Planning Association, 1991.

Richards, Anne. *The Benefits of Free Trade: East Asia and Latin America.* Paris: Organization for Economic Cooperation and Development, 1994.

Rosenburg, Jerry Martin. *The New American Community: A Response to the European and Asian Economic Challenge.* New York: Praeger, 1992.

Rugman, Alan. *Foreign Investment and NAFTA.* Columbia: University of South Carolina Press, 1994.

Tsunekawa, Keiichi. *NAFTA's Impact on Japan.* Washington, D.C.: Woodrow Wilson International Center for Scholars, 1994.

Weintraub, Sidney. *NAFTA: What Comes Next?* Westport, Conn.: Praeger, 1994.

——————— (ed.). *Integrating the Americas: Shaping Future Trade Policy.* New Brunswick, N.J.: Transaction Books, 1994.

Wonnacott, Renald J.. *The Economics of Overlapping Free Trade Areas and the Mexican Challenge.* Toronto and Washington, D.C.: Canadian American Committees, 1991.

U.S. CONGRESS

House Committee on Banking, Finance, and Urban Affairs, Subcommittee on International Development, Finance, Trade and Monetary Policy. *United States Border Environment Agreement.* Washington, D.C.: U.S. Government Printing Office, 1994.

Senate Committee on Environment and Public Works. *The North American Free Trade Agreement and Its Environmental Side Agreements. Hearings.* Washington, D.C.: U.S. Government Printing Office, 1994.

OF MORE GENERAL INTEREST

Baldwin, David A. *Economic Statecraft.* Princeton: Princeton University Press, 1985.

Doran, Charles F. *Systems in Crisis: New Imperatives of High Politics at Century's End.* Cambridge: Cambridge University Press, 1991.

Frieden, Jeffry A., and Lake, David A. (eds.). *International Political Economy: Perspectives on Global Power and Wealth.* 3rd ed. New York: St. Martins Press, 1995.

Gilpin, Robert. *The Political Economy of International Relations.* Princeton: Princeton University Press, 1987.

Ikenberry, G. John; Lake, David A; and Mastanduno, Michael (eds.). *The State and American Foreign Economic Policy.* Ithaca: Cornell, 1988.

Katzenstein, Peter (ed.). *Between Power and Plenty: Foreign Economic Policies of Advanced Industrial States.* Madison: University of Wisconsin Press, 1978.

Krasner, Steven D. *Defending the National Interest: Raw Materials Investments and U.S. Foreign Policy.* Princeton: Princeton University Press, 1978.

Keohane, Robert. *After Hegemony Cooperation and Discord in the World Economy.* Princeton: Princeton University Press, 1984.

Ruggie, John Gerald (ed.). *Multilateralism Matters.* New York: Columbia University Press, 1993.

Strange, Susan. *States and Markets.* 2nd ed. London: Pinter, 1994.

Index

About the Contributors

M. DELAL BAER is Senior Fellow and Director, Mexico Project, Center for Strategic and International Studies, Washington, D.C.

KEITH G. BANTING is Director, School of Policy Studies, and Professor of Political Science, Queens University, Kingston, Ontario.

CHARLES F. DORAN is Andrew W. Mellon Professor of International Relations, the Nitze School of Advanced International Studies (SAIS), Johns Hopkins University, Washington, D.C. He is Director of the Center of Canadian Studies and Co-Director of the North American Studies Program at SAIS.

ALVIN PAUL DRISCHLER is International Affairs Advisor to the Chairman of the Leucadia National Corporation, Washington, D.C. He is Co-Director of the North American Studies Program at SAIS, where he is a Professorial Lecturer teaching a course on the politics of international investment and political risk analysis.

RAFAEL FERNANDEZ DE CASTRO is Director of International Studies, Instituto Tecnologico Autonomo de Mexico, Mexico City.

CLAUDIA IBARGUEN is a Senior Fellow at Instituto Tecnologico Autonomo de Mexico.

A. EDWARD SAFARIAN is Senior Fellow of the Centre for International Studies, and Professor of Business Economics, University of Toronto. He is an Associate of the Canadian Institute for Advanced Research.

SIDNEY WEINTRAUB is the William E. Simon Professor in International Political Economy, Center for Strategic and International Studies, Washington, D.C.

ISBN 0-275-95406-4

HARDCOVER BAR CODE